Elder Care

This book is presented to the Montrose Regional Library
by the Montrose Rotary Club in honor of

Eva Veitch, Volunteers of America

who served as guest speaker on

May 1, 2012

Elder Care
What to Look For,
What to Look Out For!

Third Edition, Revised and Updated

Thomas M. Cassidy

New Horizon Press
Far Hills, NJ

Requests for permission should be addressed to:
New Horizon Press
P.O. Box 669
Far Hills, NJ 07931

Cassidy, Thomas M.
        Elder Care:
        What to Look For, What to Look Out For!
        Third Edition, Revised and Updated

Library of Congress Catalog Card Number: 2003114430

ISBN: 0-88282-246-2

Interior Design: Susan Sanderson
Jacket Design: Norma Ehrler Rahn
New Horizon Press
Manufactured in the U.S.A.

2008   2007   2006   2005   2004   /   6   5   4   3   2   1

Dedication

To the memory of my brother Hugh J.B. Cassidy III, who followed his dream from the playgrounds of Stuyvesant Town in Manhattan to the National Horse Show in Madison Square Garden. Hugh accepted the challenge of being a professional horseman and was an inspiration to me and our brothers, John Brendon and Joseph Patrick.

To my parents: Elizabeth Meade-Cassidy and Hugh J.B. Cassidy

To my wife: "Lee" Breen Cassidy

To our children: Brendon, Kieran, and Sean Cassidy; Sean, Kevin, and Norah Breen

To John, Suzanne, Cameron, and Emma Cassidy

To Joseph, Claudia, Ryan and Timothy Cassidy

To my cousins: Mary, Grace, and their mother, Rita Meade Arre

Author's Note

This book is based on both my experience and extensive interviews with experts, senior citizens, and their families. In order to protect the privacy and identity of others, I have changed some people's and institutions' names and identifying characteristics.

Contents

About the Author

While conducting investigations of health fraud and patient abuse as an investigator for the New York State Attorney General's Medicaid Fraud Control Unit, Thomas M. Cassidy recognized that there was a link between greed and elder abuse. *Elder Care: What To Look For, What To Look Out For!* was written to share with you the insights on elder care issues gained from his experience as an investigator and economist.

He is currently a research fellow at the American Institute for Economic Research in Great Barrington, Massachusetts, where he conducts research and analysis on senior issues, health care financing and long-term care. He is an expert in Medicare, Medicaid, Social Security and long-term care.

Tom Cassidy has published articles in the *Washington Post, San Francisco Chronicle, Dallas Morning News, Philadelphia Inquirer, San Diego Union Tribune, Star-Ledger, Hartford Courant, Investor's Business Daily, Seattle Times, Arizona Republic, Daily Oklahoman, Journal News, Buffalo News, The Bottom Line, Tomorrow* and *Personal Financial Planning.* His expertise has been cited in *Kiplinger's Retirement Report,* the *Christian Science Monitor* and in Jane Bryant Quinn's nationally syndicated column.

He holds a B.A. in history and an M.A. in economic policy analysis, both from the State University of New York (SUNY) at Stony Brook.

Tom has appeared on NBC's *Today,* CNN, FOX Network News, PBS, USA Radio Network and other television and radio programs across the country.

Tom lives in Setauket, New York with his wife, Lee.

Acknowledgments

First and foremost, I want to express my deep gratitude to senior Americans. Without your sacrifices and contributions, we in the United States would not enjoy the freedom and prosperity we have today.

Many thanks to my family, especially to my wife Lee for her encouragement and support. I owe a special debt of gratitude to my father, Hugh J.B. Cassidy, who spent many hours working with me on every phase of this book.

My friend Fred Heinze generously shared with me his personal insights on elder care. It was during conversations with Fred that I first realized that my experience could be a valuable tool to help patients and families avoid being victims of patient abuse, fraud and neglect.

It was my privilege to work for many years under the leadership of Special Prosecutors Charles "Joe" Hynes and Edward J. Kuriansky, whose tireless efforts laid the foundation for national recognition of the emerging problem of elder abuse.

Thanks to those who helped me with the development of this book, especially Richard Morrissey, Steve Kogan, Kathy MacSorley, Leonard M. Greene, Deborah Hecht, Helen Gibbs and Thomas C. Jackson.

A special thank you to three former FBI Agents: my former Chief Investigator, the late Warren J. Donovan; my immediate supervisor for almost twenty years, Anthony J. Scuderi; and my long time "partner," Bernard T. Fusco.

I also wish to thank all the members of the Long Island Office with whom I had the privilege of working from 1976 through 1996, especially Francis A. Keenan and Thomas McBride.

Prologue

When the family of Alice Baxter, a ninety-four-year-old Alzheimer's patient, hired fifty-five-year-old Fredericka Martin, a home care worker, she seemed patient and kind. The first few times Alice's granddaughter Susan and grandson Matthew came to visit, Alice was well-kept and even had a pink ribbon in her white hair. They had been concerned about their grandmother, a widow who lived alone in an upper middle class neighborhood, but Mrs. Martin's sweet, patient and caring demeanor put their minds at ease.

A few weeks later, they were dismayed to find that their grandmother's phone number had been changed to a new, unlisted number. Concerned about her well-being, Susan and Matthew went to see their grandmother. When they arrived, they were met by Mrs. Martin who told them their grandmother was sleeping. She also explained that it was she who had changed the number because she was concerned about their grandmother's health. As she told them, Alice's naps and hygiene were being constantly interrupted by phone calls from family and friends. Matt and Susan did not feel they had anything to worry about when it came to Mrs. Martin; they trusted her to make the right healthcare decisions for their grandmother. After all, she said she was a registered home health aide. So, they accepted her explanation about the telephone number and even agreed to reduce the number of visits to their ailing grandmother.

All the while, Matt, Susan and the rest of their family did not suspect what was really happening to their beloved grandmother. After cutting her off from family and friends, Fredericka Martin was little by little relieving Alice of her life savings. Mrs. Martin carefully looted Alice's bank accounts and stocks. She spent several hundred thousand dollars immediately and allocated even larger sums to her family members and to her own bank account.

But Alice's life savings were not enough for the greedy criminal. After almost two years of bilking Alice, Fredericka Martin perpetrated a major scam. Hiring Carrie Bellows, a small-time actress and petty criminal, Martin dressed her up as Alice, complete with pink ribbon. The two met with bank representatives and forged the documents necessary to put Alice Baxter's home of forty years in Martin's name. Then they met with a real estate agent and put the house on the market. Within a few weeks, Bellows was posed once again as Alice, pink ribbon and all, for the sale of the home. And so, without Alice Baxter's consent or her family's knowledge, the home was sold and the two con-women walked away with almost one hundred thousand dollars.

Although the IRS had become suspicious of Fredericka Martin, it was too late for Alice Baxter and her family. It wasn't until Mrs. Martin was arrested that Alice's family learned the painful and horrifying truth. Their penniless, dazed, malnourished grandmother was found in an apartment in a seedy neighborhood while a new family lived happily in her home. In the end, Alice Baxter was placed in a nursing home at a great cost to her family and almost all of her savings and assets—estimated to be worth approximately one million dollars—had been stolen.

 Introduction

Elderly women who live alone and patients who suffer from Alzheimer's and other forms of dementia are especially susceptible to suffering the same fate as Alice Baxter at the hands of an unscrupulous person. In particular, Alzheimer's patients may not be capable of reporting crimes to law enforcement officials. In addition, because of the nature of this type of illness, their complaints are sometimes ignored by their families and friends. For the shrewd and devious, senior women living alone are vulnerable and easy targets because they often cannot defend themselves physically. And like many healthy, senior Americans—including men—they are reluctant to report cases of fraud and abuse. Rosalie S. Wolfe, president of the National Committee for the Prevention of Elder Abuse, offers this explanation: "Some frail, older persons who are mistreated by home care workers do not report the incidents to their families or the authorities. They are ashamed that they have allowed themselves to be victimized and so conceal the incidents to avoid being judged incompetent. Above all, they fear that they will no longer be able to remain at home."

For the better part of twenty years, I investigated health fraud and patient abuse for the New York State Attorney General's Medicaid Fraud Control Unit. As an investigator, I saw firsthand the tragedies that can occur when elderly patients are abused, defrauded, or neglected. I also observed that elder fraud cases, once a rarity, are on the rise. One thing is true in every case of elder fraud and abuse: caregivers take advantage of their position of trust. As the senior population increases, accumulates more wealth and becomes more and more dependent on others, the potential for elder fraud and abuse will rise dramatically and the methods used to commit crimes against the elderly will become more various and elaborate. It is vital that family and friends with elder care concerns be very careful and consult with trained health care professionals, remain actively involved in every aspect of care and make frequent unannounced visits.

No one can predict with any accuracy the day and time when a serious illness or injury will strike. But we can insulate ourselves from fraud and abuse if we make plans **and** take the necessary steps while we are healthy. Not every crime can be avoided, but we can reduce the risk of elder fraud, abuse and neglect if we plan ahead and use every available resource to help those who helped us. *Elder Care: What To Look For, What To Look Out For!* was written to share with you the insights on elder care issues derived from my experience as an investigator, researcher and economist. *Elder Care* is designed to empower **all** Americans and their families with the message that they can avoid the peril of elder fraud and abuse if they take protective steps while they are healthy. Each chapter of this book will alert you to some of the potential problems faced by older Americans and give resources to help you make a defensive plan.

By far the worst cases of elder abuse I ever saw or heard of involved vulnerable patients who were placed in the hands of *illegal and unlicensed* elder care providers who charged less than half the cost of their licensed competitors. What kind of person would allow older relatives to be placed in an illegal or "underground" nursing home? The answer is: all kinds of people—spouses, adult children, nieces, nephews and even the patients themselves—all of whom faced the same dilemma. Medicare did not cover the patient's nursing home care and he or she was not poor enough to qualify for Medicaid. Without any long-term care insurance and desperate to preserve a lifetime of savings, they used poor judgement. In this situation, relatives preoccupied with preserving a patient's estate may make decisions that result in unnecessary pain, suffering and even death for their "loved" ones.

Similarly, too many elders are placed in the care of unreliable and unlicensed home care providers who offer seemingly bargain-priced care. These arrangements are a bad deal at best and the results can be truly tragic—as was the cruel reality for a ninety-year-old woman who was robbed and beaten by an *unlicensed* home health aide. In this case, the home care aide had been independently hired; that is, not found through an agency or other authorized and monitored source.

The stress and shock of learning that Medicare does not cover long-term care, prescription drugs and numerous other health services may make the many older Americans who have planned poorly or not at all for these expenses more vulnerable to predatory caregivers. All too often, it is only at the last minute, when weakened and dependent patients are discharged from the hospital, that they and their families realize that the entire financial burden of long term care now falls on them alone. Most older patients do receive compassionate care from their caregivers, but the financial burden of providing dependent care is often a contributing factor in elder abuse and neglect, either directly (overt abuse) or indirectly (inability or unwillingness to pay for caregiving services). Moreover, many older people have pensions, investment income, or other significant wealth and sadly this has caught the greedy eye of a new category of thief.

To be effective, undercover investigators and informants are trained by law enforcement agencies to gain the trust of the targeted individual. The same strategy is used by the crooks who prey on our senior population. It is important to remember that their purpose is to deceive. They are proficient at disguising their motives and may *appear* to be the most compassionate of caregivers. As an investigator, I met firsthand many elder abusers. Most appeared to be kind and caring—

perfect companions for their elder patients. Many even affected an air of piety or professed to be devoutly religious to bolster the deception. There were common elements in most of these cases; the motives were usually frustration, indifference, hate and most important, *greed*. This book should serve as a wake-up call that will prompt you to use all available resources to provide superior elder care.

The best safeguard senior patients can have is the active involvement of family, friends, neighbors and the community at large. Even with the utmost vigilance, not every elder crime can be prevented. Some are spontaneous, like the slap, pinch, curse, or kick from a heartless guardian. These incidents sometimes occur in a moment of anger or personal frustration, perhaps prompted by a confused patient's act of aggression. Trained caregivers are taught to expect this type of behavior and to react calmly and appropriately. How can you guard against such incidents? In later chapters I will tell you about some danger signals to watch for.

However, seniors can also safeguard themselves by taking matters into their hands before they are frail or sick. Again, some of the most dangerous, even illegal, elder care situations are due to a lack of planning and economic burdens. If patients and their families understand their options and carefully plan for their future, they can protect themselves financially, physically and emotionally. For example, seniors must anticipate all of the expenses associated with both the care they expect or hope to have (e.g. home care) and the higher level of care they may be forced to utilize (e.g. a nursing home). Although the costs of different levels of care vary, none are inexpensive. Medicare may pay for some of the portable medical equipment needed for home care, but it does not pay for long-term care. An assisted living residence may sound appealing, but most of the time, individuals privately pay without any assistance from Medicare or Medicaid. A nursing home may be required at some point; however, this type of care comes at a great expense to the patient, starting at around $50,000 a year and rising. It is easy to see why it is so important to carefully plan for future expenses.

The purpose of *Elder Care* is to alert readers to the potential peril that a defenseless patient might encounter, teach how to avoid being a victim of elder abuse and show how to protect loved ones. This book lists referrals and a comprehensive personal worksheet to record the vital information needed in case of an emergency. *Elder Care* will also provide in-depth advice from the experts interviewed: Dr. Lynn Tepper, who holds a Doctorate in Gerontology from Columbia University; Kathy Adams-Simmers, a Certified Public Accountant and Partner in the firm of Jaskot and Adams; and Steven M. Cohen, Esq., an attorney and partner in the law firm of Lorenzo and Cohen in Buffalo, NY. Their insights are invaluable.

Let's work together to address your concerns and those of your loved ones. If a family member or friend is assisting with the care of an older loved one, this book will help them start solving his or her problems now. For those who are healthy, *Elder Care* will help to start planning and investing in the future.

I have the experience to help you and I want to share it.

 Chapter 1

Elder Fraud:
Isolation Can Lead to Exploitation

Elder fraud cases were once a rarity. This is no longer the case. Older people, many of whom have pensions, life savings and other sources of significant wealth, have caught the attention of professional con-artists who fleece the elderly for a living. They prey on elders who are isolated and/or homebound, then scheme a strategy to steal their money and valuables. Sadly, the money that is stolen from elderly victims often deprives them of the opportunity to live comfortably in their retirement years, or is part of a bequest they intend to leave to relatives and friends, as well as their church, temple or other charitable institutions.

This new, particularly despicable breed of thief attempts to maintain continuous access to the elderly, by befriending their targets and waiting for responses from relatives or friends. If the "coast is clear," and there are no reactions from others, the fraud accelerates. Isolation can lead to exploitation, especially among senior citizens.

It is important to realize that most thieves are proficient at disguising their motives. For example, one team of bandits that preyed on the elderly posed as utility workers to gain entrance to their homes. One thief would then distract the victim by talking about a water emergency in the neighborhood, while the other ransacked the bedrooms, stealing all the cash, jewelry and other valuables that he could find.

Not all elder frauds are this well-planned or elaborate. Some thefts occur simply because trusting people leave valuables unguarded, as was the case of an older woman who routinely was robbed by her cleaning person. Over the course of the year many different repairmen, delivery persons or home care workers may have unsupervised access to the home of a trusting elderly person. Minimizing possible temptation and opportunity can help keep these people honest and prevent theft.

Telemarketing Fraud

Not all elder frauds are committed in the home. It is estimated that telemarketing fraud robs Americans of more than $40 billion annually. AARP found that 56 percent of the names of victims on "mooch lists" (what fraudulent telemarketers call their lists of most likely victims) were age fifty or older. The FBI estimates that about 14,000 illegal telemarketing operations are bilking consumers every day. Older people are often the target of these operations, partly because due to stronger belief systems, many elders feel that it is impolite to hang up on a caller. However, we should all be aware that when a stranger calls asking for money, even if it seems to be for a charitable organization, he or she could be a crook.

Do not furnish any personal information should you receive such calls and ask to be placed on their "do-not-call" list. For your own protection, hang up as quickly as possible. One ninety-year-old woman could have avoided a serious problem if she had hung up on a telemarketer who offered her free burial space, on the condition that she allow a salesperson to visit her at home. The visit proved very costly and she was duped into purchasing an $11,000 crypt. The financing arrangements included 99 payments and additional finance charges of well over $7,000.

One way to reduce the possibility of being a victim of a telemarketing fraud is to have your phone number placed on the do-not-call registry at the state and federal level. The Federal Trade Commission has recently created a national do-not-call registry (1-800-382-1222) allowing citizens to prevent telemarketing both legal and illegal. It is illegal and punishable with serious fines for most telemarketers to call any number listed on the registry.

Internet Fraud

The Internet is another place where older consumers are at risk for fraud and deception. Law enforcement agencies at the state and federal level are working together with consumer protection organizations from around the world in "Operation Top Ten Dot Cons" to combat Internet fraud. Many Internet crooks target older consumers. For example, health frauds claim to provide miracle products and treatments that cure any number of serious illnesses and are not sold through traditional suppliers. Similarly, financial schemes involving fraudulent off shore accounts that require the victim to give a bank account number are increasingly common. We all must take steps to protect ourselves from high-tech con artists who are using clever schemes in their attempts to defraud consumers-particularly the elderly.

There is free information available from the Federal Trade Commission (FTC) to help consumers spot, stop and avoid fraud by calling 1-800-382-4357. In addition, if you or someone you know is a victim of telemarketing, Internet, credit card, identity or any other type of fraud, contact the FTC as soon as possible.

Identity Theft and Financial Fraud

Although electronic banking and credit cards offer unimaginable convenience, they also offer the criminal opportunities for fraud. The recent arrest of a woman accused of stealing the identities of her elderly victims to apply for credit cards for her own use is only one story in an ever-growing list of crime. This fraud was uncovered by observant postal workers; other elderly victims are not always so fortunate.

It is important that consumers monitor their mail to make certain they receive their routine monthly bank or credit card statements listing recent transactions. Don't just throw them in a drawer unread; check for unusual or unauthorized activity. Although you can't prevent identity theft entirely, there are steps that you can take to minimize your risk. Shredding your junk mail, such as pre-approved credit card mailings, as well as any of your financial records, before you put them in the trash will stop thieves who steal identities by sorting through garbage and dumpsters.

However, all consumers must understand that no matter how well they protect their mail, telephone and Internet transactions, they are still at risk for identity theft. We all are. For example, consider the recent arrest of a software employee who stole the credit histories of 30,000 people and sold them to a ring of thieves. It could take years for some of these victims to discover that their identities have been stolen.

If you suspect that your identity has been stolen, immediately file a complaint with the FTC by contacting the FTC Identity Theft Hotline toll-free at: 1-877-IDTHEFT (438-4338). In addition, the FTC suggests that you order a copy of your credit report from each of the three major credit reporting agencies every year. Make sure these reports are accurate and include only those activities you have authorized. The law allows credit bureaus to charge you up to $9.00 for a copy of your credit report.

Credit Bureaus

Equifax: http://www.equifax.com
To order your report, call: 1-800-685-1111
or write: P.O. Box 740241, Atlanta, GA 30374-0241
To report fraud, call: 1-800-525-6285
and write: P.O. Box 740241, Atlanta, GA 30374-0241

Experian: http://www.experian.com
To order your report, call: 1-888-EXPERIAN (397-3742)
or write: P.O. Box 2104, Allen TX 75013

To report fraud, call: 1–888–EXPERIAN (397–3742)
and write: P.O. Box 9532, Allen TX 75013

TransUnion: http://www.transunion.com
To order your report, call: 800–916–8800
or write: P.O. Box 1000, Chester, PA 19022.
To report fraud, call: 1–800–680–7289
and write: Fraud Victim Assistance Division, P.O. Box 6790, Fullerton, CA 92634

Home Improvement Fraud

Fraudulent home improvement contractors often target older consumers. The elderly have a greater need for home improvements than the average person. They tend to live in older homes which need more repairs and they are less able to do repairs themselves generally.

A thirty-three year-old con man who was sent to jail for swindling seven elderly victims out of $60,000 is just one example of an unlicensed home contractor with a plan to steal from the elderly. His first step was to frighten his victims by telling them they had a dangerous carbon monoxide build up in their chimney and they could die if he didn't fix it. Then he took their money and did no work, simply disappearing. As the AARP warns consumers, "The person who shows up at your front door offering to do work for you is rarely the right choice."

It is important for older consumers to choose the right contractor for any repair or home improvement. An important first step is to get some recommendations from people you know and trust, along with proof that the contractor is licensed, bonded, covered by worker's compensation and liability insurance. It is wise to make a list of the specific things you want a contractor to repair or maintain. As a general rule, the more that you know about the person you've hired at the beginning of any project, the better off you will be when the project ends.

Investment Fraud

Retirees who are worried about meeting their future income needs are especially vulnerable to get rich quick schemes. Often these scams are the work of unlicensed agents who lure older investors with what they call "sure deals." The guilty plea of a scam artist who admitted stealing $1.8 million by persuading investors, all of whom ranged from age sixty to eighty, to leave their conservative investments for his supposedly lucrative, but actually worthless scheme, is just one example of the investment fraud that is commonly perpetrated against the elderly.

Always make certain that the person selling you securities is licensed, but don't stop there. Never let anyone, whether licensed or not, pressure or scare you into making a quick decision. All consumers, especially the elderly, should be cautious whenever they receive an offer that sounds too good to be true and must be taken advantage of immediately. Take your time and make certain that the recommended investments are registered with appropriate government regulators and are suitable for your age, income, assets, needs, goals and risk tolerance. It is a good idea to discuss any potential investment with trusted family members and professional advisors like certified public accountants and attorneys, before any serious decision is made.

How to Prevent Elder Fraud

Encouragingly, fraud and financial exploitation are often preventable, especially when we remove the temptation to steal before a problem arises. As friends and family members, we must not simply assume that our elderly relatives and friends have taken all the necessary steps to protect themselves from the startling array of predators. Make sure that all cash, jewelry, financial records, checkbooks and credit cards are safeguarded in a protected location such as a safe or safe deposit box, especially if an elderly person's home is highly trafficked by non-friends and strangers. Arrangements should be made so that social security, pension and investment checks are direct-deposited into bank accounts to prevent theft and forgery. Monitor the mail to make certain routine monthly financial statements listing recent transactions are received.

Remember, as devious as are these many schemes, thieves preying on the elderly can be stopped by alert consumers with a plan.

What to Do

As a former senior investigator specializing in crimes against the elderly, my recommendation for those who suspect that they, or elder relatives or friends, have been victims of fraud, is to take action as soon as possible. Here's what to do.

Write It Down. It is helpful, if you suspect that something is wrong, to write it down on paper. Always include the date, time, place and witnesses, along with details of your observations. This type of information may prove helpful at a later date. Take for example, the case of elder crime in which a seventy-five-year-old woman was robbed and terrorized in her own home by an opportunistic thief. She had the presence of mind to write a detailed five-page account of her ordeal. The woman then contacted the police and reported the crime. The detectives, armed with this information, were quickly able to arrest the suspect.

Call the Police

In case of an emergency, call 911. Never hesitate to call the police if you suspect a crime has been committed. They want to help. The sooner they arrive on the scene, the better the chance that a case can be solved.

 Chapter 2

Unacceptable Risk:
The Unlicensed Caregiver

It is human nature, particularly in today's economic climate, to try and cut costs. Unfortunately, elder care and bottom of the barrel prices are often not compatible. The use of unlicensed providers who entice clients with "bargain-priced" care can lead to tragedy. When you hire from the unlicensed, uncertified, underground pool of caregivers, your chances of having a serious problem increase exponentially. The risk to health and wealth is far greater and the results can be tragic. The all too frequently occurring arrests of people accused of stealing from elderly home care patients are cases in point. Horror stories abound: in one of these cases, an unlicensed home care worker who was on disability leave continued to pose as a home care attendant for her ninety-seven-year-old and ninety-one-year-old married patients. This imposter allegedly stole more than $300,000 over the course of a year by systematically stealing the bulk of her patients' life savings. Many older Americans who need long-term care but rely on unlicensed workers are at risk for this type of fraud.

Chronic illness is expensive. The long-term care patient needs the help of others each and every day. That costs a lot of money. Medicare does not cover long-term care. For many Americans who have planned poorly or not at all for such expenses this causes unexpected stress. Too often, a patient does not learn until they are discharged from a hospital that he or she has to bear the total financial burden of the payment of home care, assisted-living residence fees or nursing home costs.

An unscrupulous thief needs only one chance to steal from a trusting client. For example, consider this case of elder fraud in which a theft was uncovered by the relatives of an elderly patient on the very first day after a home care worker was hired. Two rings valued at $2,450 each and $1,073 in cash had been stolen from the home. This same person, they later learned, had been charged with similar thefts in a neighboring county and state. Such are the risks of hiring unregistered "professionals."

As an investigator, I had the opportunity to meet and hear the experiences of thousands of chronically ill patients and their caregivers in their homes, assisted-living residences or nursing homes. As a result of my professional experience, friends and family began to ask me for advice when they faced concerns about their elderly loved ones. I listened to their predicaments and tried to guide them to the resources appropriate for their particular problem. My long experience led me to caution each of them to be very careful, avoid shortcuts and always use the services of trained, licensed professionals.

When you need to hire a caregiver it is always important to hire licensed and/or certified agencies or individuals who are overseen and regulated by government agencies. The following important steps can reduce the opportunity for fraud.

Careful selection of the homecare worker is crucial. Limit your options to home care agencies that are licensed and/or certified by the state. If you hire an independent contractor, make certain that he or she is licensed and registered with the state. It is absolutely vital to verify all licenses with the authorized regulatory agencies before you hire a caregiver.

It is most important to make certain that the homecare worker is compatible with the patient. Screen all home care workers, interviewing them thoroughly before allowing them to meet their potential patient.

Request a change of staff if you are not satisfied with any employee, whether you are paying the agency directly or the agency is being paid by a third party, such as Medicare, Medicaid or a private insurer.

Additionally:
- Check references of both the agency and individual employees.
- Don't pay off the books; pay by check or credit card so that you have a backup receipt for your own records.
- Make random, unannounced visits to observe the treatment that the patient is receiving and pay careful attention to any signs of fear or abuse in the patient.
- Inventory and safeguard valuables before you hire a homecare worker. Similarly, safeguard all financial records.
- Have pension, investment and social security checks direct-deposited into accounts to avoid forgeries.
- Restrict access of home care workers to the patient area. This will assist the police in the event there is a theft, since a home care worker's fingerprints and other evidence should be limited to a specific area.

The Illegal Nursing Home

The dark curtains in this residence for the elderly were always drawn. Visiting hours were restricted to Saturdays from 10:00 a.m. to noon, and patients were warned that their conversations were being recorded. The cost for this illegal nursing home was only a third of what was charged by the licensed operators in the area, where a one-year stay might easily run $90,000 or more.

Confronted with such expenses, individuals and their families attempting to preserve savings or an estate may be driven to extreme measures, sometimes even placing vulnerable older patients in the care of underground, "off the books" unlicensed providers who offer inferior care at a bargain price. Such bargains, though, always prove costly in the long term.

In this case, the illegal nursing home was run by a high school dropout. She wore a white nursing uniform, though her only nursing experience was as an aide at a state psychiatric hospital. To all who met her, she seemed sincere and caring. Her motive, however, was greed.

Some of her patients suffered from severe dementia. One such patient was an older man suffering from Alzheimer's Disease who previously had been residing in an assisted-living facility. Reported missing and the object of an intense police search, he had walked almost four miles before he was finally found by a night shift employee on his way to work. When the incident convinced the assisted-living facility that the patient needed more supervision than they could provide, his wife placed him in the care of this unlicensed nursing home. He was confined to his bed both day and night, shackled by ankle and wrist restraints. After a few months, the problem of his wandering away became a moot point. Even when unshackled, he could go nowhere. His joints had calcified and he could no longer walk.

Analysis

You must be observant before you choose a health care facility, especially if you are acting on behalf of a relative or friend. When looking for a nursing home, the federal government provides an extremely helpful website at http://www.medicare.gov. This site provides detailed information about the performance of every Medicare and Medicaid certified nursing home in the United States. Other resources at this site include the "Guide To Choosing a Nursing Home" and a "Nursing Home Checklist.". It is important to find licensed and/or certified facilities that are known to government agencies. This web site and the steps that follow will provide you with a starting point in your search for a nursing home suitable to care for your loved one.

What to Look For
•   Licensed and certified facilities that are regulated by government

agencies should be the only facilities you consider. For example, in many states the health department routinely inspects nursing homes to ensure that the facility complies with acceptable sanitary standards. Often health departments employ nurses who visit patients at nursing homes. These nurse are trained to look for any indication of abuse.

- Review the regulatory inspection reports that are submitted by administrative agencies, both public and private.
- The Ombudsman's Office is a service financed by the federal government that is designed to assist people with problems relating to nursing homes. Contact your state or local Department of Aging to obtain information about the ombudsman and other important information. A list of each state's Department of Aging is included in the appendix.
- Make an unannounced visit and request a tour of the home. Pay attention to details, the attitude of the staff and the health and happiness of the patients. Are there activities and volunteers? Do you see smiles?
- Visit more than one nursing home so that you have a basis for accurate comparison.
- Contact your patient's doctor regarding any healthcare setting.
- Don't switch doctors unless absolutely necessary.

What to Look Out For
- Beware of bargain rates; elder care is never on sale. As an investigator, I found that almost every fraud appealed to the bank account. The con game is played every day and the victim is usually looking for a deal.
- Avoid any facilities that are not known to the Department of Aging or other government agencies. Be careful of hidden residences that are secluded from the public view and are not visibly identified as a health care facility either at the location or in the phone book.
- Restricted visitation could indicate that there may be something

to hide. A nursing home should allow visitors on a daily basis. They may, however, impose reasonable restrictions on visiting hours to coordinate the personal hygiene of patients. Regardless, a family or friend should be able to make arrangements with the administration when the posted hours are not compatible with the visitor's schedule. Remember, often there are several patients in each room at a nursing home, therefore visitors may be restricted from a patient's room at the request of a roommate.

 Chapter 3

Long-term Care: More than Just Nursing Homes

The world of elder care is a rapidly developing one and offers great benefits to those who are prepared for the challenges and stresses, but can be stressful and confusing for those who are not. To begin with, it is very emotional for elders when they realize that they are no longer a tower of strength and that they need help. Often they rely upon their adult children to assist them with care giving decisions, an uncomfortable role reversal for many family members. Compounding this problem, there are often emotional, psychological and financial stresses for both the patient and the caregiver.

Although a majority of our elders spend their later years in relatively good health, not every older person enjoys an independent and healthy elderly life. Some develop chronic conditions requiring the assistance of caregivers, either temporarily or for the rest of their lives. Statistically, it is more likely that as a person ages, he or she will need long-term care. This loss of independence can be a painful reality for many previously healthy and independent older Americans, but those who remain in denial of their potential need for long-term care hurt themselves in the long run.

Home Care: Safety First

Most older men and women want to remain in their own homes as
long as possible. It should be our goal to help them achieve this goal
with the peace of mind that comes from living in a safe and secure
home. The National Center for Injury Prevention and Control esti-
mates that each year in the United States, one in three people older
than age sixty-five suffers a significant fall. Fortunately, many falls and
injuries can be prevented when a meaningful effort is made to create a
safe environment. The old proverb, "an ounce of prevention is worth a
pound of cure," is especially true for older persons.

A fall can cause serious injury and may push an older person
to a chronic or even permanent need for a higher level of care. For
example, half the elderly patients hospitalized for hip fracture cannot
return home or live independently after the fracture. But there are many
practical ways to increase the safety of any home and often the only
cost is time. For example, removing hazards such as small step-stools,
loose rugs, electrical cords and other potential dangers can reduce the
possibility of a serious fall.

Recently, while visiting a ninety-one year-old friend, my wife
Lee noticed a tear in the living room rug. For a healthy person this
might not pose a threat, but for a ninety-one year-old, who has failing
eyesight and uses a walker, it poses a real and significant danger. The
rug was repaired immediately, perhaps averting a serious fall.

There are many ways to increase the safety and security of our
elders. Some are as simple as installing brighter lights in the home to
compensate for failing eyesight, or providing night lights to mark a clear
path to the bathroom in the dark. Other preventative measures include
installing smoke detectors throughout the home, especially in the
kitchen. Installing a burglar alarm system can add to the safety of an
elder, especially if the system includes a medical alert feature which can
be activated with a remote. Portable and cellular phones can facilitate
emergency calls, not to mention making it easier for the older person
to keep in touch with family and friends. Another great idea would be

to modify or possibly remodel the bathroom, adding safety features such as handrails, grab-bars, non-slip floors, or mats in tubs or shower stalls. Beyond the immediate safety benefits, the peace of mind offered by such simple adjustments is immeasurable to both the elderly and their family and loved ones.

Long-term Care: It's Not Just for the Elderly

Dr. Anthony Frasca, a Yale-trained anesthesiologist, was only forty-five years old when he decided to have surgery on the herniated disc in his lower spine. As a doctor, he had firsthand knowledge of the procedure and all of its complications. After the surgery, while lying in the recovery room, he asked the nurse three questions. Why am I shaking? Why am I paralyzed? Why am I asking you questions I already know the answers to?

The following day, when the surgeon arrived, she helped him get out of bed and he was able to support his weight with her help. Although she was encouraged by his progress, she did not know how long he would be paralyzed from the waist down. He was discharged from the hospital the next day. His wife, Andrea, a professional nurse, was his caregiver. There were days when he would slide out of bed and lie on the floor. He hoped he could crawl to his walker, but he could only lie in pain on the floor. Fortunately for Dr. Frasca, he responded positively to physical therapy and was able to return to work on a part-time basis eight months after his surgery. It took another year before he could work a full week.

Dr. Frasca had an insurance policy that provided him with income during his disability and his wife, a nurse, was able to provide him care (otherwise he would have had to use his disability income to pay for a caregiver) and he responded to therapy. Not everyone is as fortunate. More than twelve million Americans need some form of long-term care. While most are elderly, forty percent are not. It is not a possibility that most plan for, but it is important to be prepared in the event of the unthinkable occurring.

Home Health Care: Make Plans Now

Many costly and sometimes even tragic mistakes are made when a patient is being discharged from a hospital and they are under pressure to make quick decisions about future care. As someone who investigated fraud cases for almost twenty years, I know firsthand the value of having a home health care plan in place before it is needed. Your plan can include the possibility of receiving care from your spouse, family and friends if home help is ever needed. Keep in mind that as we age, our children age with us, which is why one home health aide I know is caring for both an eighty-nine year-old mother and her sixty-nine year old daughter.

Elder care plans should include the possibility of hiring home care workers. You can hire home care workers independently, use an agency specializing in home health care, or use some combination of both choices (review chapter 5, Home Care, as you develop your plan).

Home Care: Medicare Does Help

Although Medicare does not pay for long-term custodial care, it does help to pay for much of the portable equipment needed by a patient to remain at home. This equipment is usually covered by Medicare after the deductible has been met and is subject to the 20 percent Medicare co-payment.

Remodel or Retrofit for Home Care Needs

In addition to medical and healthcare expenses, a home might require an expensive renovation or addition in order to be practical for home care, both costly changes. It may be years away or it may never happen, but it is still wise to plan now for the possibility of converting or adding a bedroom and bathroom on the ground level.

My parents live in a two-level home with the bedrooms and full-size bathrooms on the second floor. A few years ago, my mother developed painful arthritis which made it difficult for her to climb stairs. She approached this problem in two steps. Her first step was to purchase a treadmill and begin a physician-supervised rehabilitation program. Step two involved a well-thought-out decision by my parents to remodel their home rather than move into a condominium or senior residence. They met with a reputable building contractor who provided them with a cost estimate and floor plan for adding a bedroom and bathroom on the first floor. Fortunately, my mother's exercise program has relieved her arthritis pain and now, with the remodeling plan ready if needed, my parents also have peace of mind about their future. They have planned ahead and should the need arise, they can confront a change with confidence and security.

Assisted-living Facilities

Assisted-living facilities offer enormous potential benefit to the quality of life for older people but like any other major decision you have to be careful. You can't assume that because it is an appealing alternative to home care or a nursing home, you don't have to do your research. You do. Any quality facility will expect that, because they know they are going to look very good. They should not have anything to hide.

An assisted-living facility is a general term that describes a non-medical residence. This type of residence might be known in your community by any of the following names: rest home, board and care home, adult home, or senior residence. An assisted-living facility can provide a comfortable living environment for older clients, at less cost than a nursing home. As a general rule, assisted-living residences do not participate in Medicare or Medicaid and, therefore, most of their clients are private payers.

This type of residence usually provides meals, social activities, transportation and various other services. Staff members might assist residents with personal care and remind them when to take medications, but they are limited by state regulation as to which services they can provide. Assisted-living facilities are not nursing homes and, consequently, before a consumer signs an agreement, it is important to make certain that he or she understands all of the benefits as well as the limitations of this type of living arrangement. This contract is a legal document which should be reviewed by the consumer's attorney.

Nursing Homes

The time may come when a person can no longer choose the option of either home care or an assisted-living residence and must choose the higher level of care found in a skilled nursing facility, commonly known as a nursing home. Many fragile older patients require the assistance of not one, but *two* trained aides just to transfer them from bed to chair. It took two trained aides to turn a completely bedridden ninety-six year old woman whom I met at a nursing home. She had to be turned from side to side in this manner at least once every ninety minutes; otherwise, she was in excruciating pain. Even so, she told me most emphatically that she did not want to live in a nursing home. Though her sense of independence suffered, it is only in such a facility that she can receive adequate care for her remaining years.

       Nursing homes are inspected by regulatory agencies to ensure that they provide a safe environment for patients, staff and visitors. However, it is still of utmost importance to visit and tour several nursing homes before you make your choice, because there is a world of difference between a well-run nursing home and one that merely meets the minimum standards outlined by the state. In addition, as more potential consumers enter the market for nursing home care, demand may well exceed supply and quality may suffer. Therefore, the first choice may not be available at a time of crisis. Let me give you an actual example of what I mean:

       Jean was asked to help find a nursing home for a hospitalized friend. Her first choice, the nursing home where her friend's mother had been a patient, had no bed available so her friend was put on a waiting list. Jean called six more nursing homes before finally finding a facility outside of her preferred location, with an available bed. Eventually Jean's friend transferred out of that nursing home to one closer to her home. A few hours later, Jean went back to the nursing home to get her friend's clothes and found another patient already in the bed her friend had just vacated.

Continuing Care Retirement Communities

Continuing Care Retirement Communities (CCRCs) provide a continuum of service levels ranging from independent living, assisted-living and nursing home care for as long as you are a resident. It is sometimes referred to as "lifecare," since all of these services are provided by or within one community. People who consider moving into a CCRC must be careful when making a selection. Some CCRCs require consumers to pay a substantial entry fee with the assumption that they will be able to utilize an increased level of care in the future. Other CCRCs with a fee-for-service agreement charge residents a lower monthly service fee and residents are responsible for all costs of additional health care services if needed.

It is of critical importance that the CCRC resident agreement is clearly understood by the consumer, particularly if a lump-sum entry fee is an admission requirement. The financial status and reputation of the CCRC and its owners should be investigated, as well as the terms of resale, refunds, fee increases and all social and decision-making issues associated with the facility. A CCRC contract should be reviewed by the consumer's attorney, accountant and financial advisor before entering into a contract.

Helpful Resources

The appendix of this book includes the names, addresses and websites for many agencies and organizations that provide valuable elder care information. However, if you have an immediate need for elder care, the geriatric department at a reputable hospital in your community is a good place to get help. They may have geriatricians, gerontologists, nurse practitioners, geriatric social workers, nurses and other health professionals on staff who are trained to address the needs specific to older patients.

Volunteers

It is estimated that almost sixty-five percent of the home care needs for older patients living in the community are provided by unpaid caregivers. These are the spouses, adult children, relatives and friends who provide elder care for their loved ones. There are many others who are not counted in statistics. They are the volunteers who deliver meals-on-wheels, raise funds, visit or phone the homebound and those in assisted-living and nursing home facilities. These heroes provide comfort for the elderly with little thought of themselves and make the world of the elderly far brighter.

One of the many volunteers is my father, Hugh J. B. (Joe) Cassidy. He was recently awarded the "Legion of Honor of the Four Chaplains" for his commitment and dedication to the veterans who are patients at the Long Island State Veteran's Home, which is operated by the Stony Brook University Health Science Center. I would like to share with you the heroic acts of the four chaplains in World War II as reminder that people can make a difference.

On a bitterly cold morning in the North Atlantic in February 1943, the troop ship U.S.S. *Dorchester* was torpedoed as it was approaching Greenland. Many of the soldiers and sailors packed into the lower part of the ship died in the original explosion. Others, shocked and disoriented, made their way to the decks through smoke-filled passageways only to find that several lifeboats were destroyed.

The four chaplains, Rev. Clark V. Poling (Dutch Reformed), Rabbi Alexander D. Goode (Jewish), Rev. Fr. John P. Washington (Roman Catholic) and Rev. George L. Fox (Methodist) gathered on deck to rally the men. All four remained calm, assisting the troops and steeling their resolve. They gave away their own life jackets to those who had none. Then, linked arm in arm on the deck of the sinking ship, they prayed for the safety of the others. When last seen, they were still standing together as the sea closed over their heads.

My father joined the Coast Guard before his eighteenth birthday and served during World War II on the U.S.S. *Cavalier* in the South
Pacific. After his ship's fifth invasion in Subic Bay, the *Cavalier* was torpedoed and the rear of the ship was blown off. Unlike the *Dorchester*,
the ship did not sink and was towed to safety. But Joe Cassidy, the sailor,
thought of the four chaplains when his ship was disabled in the South
Pacific and he feels their spirit in every patient at the nursing home.

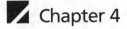 Chapter 4

Long-term Care Insurance

Long-term care is not a single, unified program of care, but is made up of many different support services aimed at helping people who have lost some capacity for self-care because of a cognitive or chronic condition or illness. These patients require the help of others to perform what are referred to as "activities of daily living" (ADL), which include eating, bathing, toileting, dressing, transferring and continence. A comprehensive long-term care insurance policy pays for care at the patient's home, in an assisted-living facility or in a nursing home. Tax qualified long-term care insurance policies will pay a claim if you are expected to need substantial assistance for at least ninety days with at least two ADLs or require substantial supervision due to severe cognitive impairment such as Alzheimer's Disease or dementia.

The time to plan for elder care is while a person is healthy and independent. No one wants to be dependent or envisions themselves in such a situation, but it is important to prepare early and well for the possibility. I have heard many people vow that they would never become a patient in a nursing home, as if, when that decision must be made, there were really any choice. Luckily, options exist today which allow many older Americans to receive care at home or in an assisted-living resi-

dence, rather than a nursing home. Such care is expensive and people
have several choices to make when paying for long-term care. You can
use your own money to pay for services, you can depend on family or
friends for help, your long-term care insurer can pay, or if you are impoverished, Medicaid, the health insurer for the poor, may pay for your care.

Rather than purchase a long-term care insurance policy, some
Americans "game" the system by transferring their money and assets
to heirs and beneficiaries in order to appear impoverished and qualify
for Medicaid. I read recently about the tragic suicide of a seventy-nine
year-old man whose attempt at "Medicaid planning" led to his death.
Let me explain:

A few years ago an elderly man transferred his assets, including his home, into his son's name, in case he should ever need to be
placed in a nursing home. Let Medicaid pay, he figured. He later
changed his mind and wanted his assets back. It took protracted litigation for the man to get his assets back from his son. But more distress-
ing for this grandfather than the litigation were the actions of his son
and daughter-in-law, who barred him from seeing his grandchildren.
Distraught and angry at his family's greed, he ultimately took his own
life.

Although we can't turn back the clock for this man and his
family, we can learn a lesson about the risks associated with "Medicaid
planning." Once you transfer control of your money, those who receive
it may not support your wishes, give the money back, invest it wisely
or even pay for your care at home or in an assisted-living facility that
does not participate in the Medicaid program.

For those who are healthy and can afford it, a long-term care
insurance policy that meets their needs and goals can be a good investment. I consider my long-term care insurance policy as a type of cata-
strophic health insurance. It has a substantial deductible (the elimination or waiting period) and a co-payment above the daily benefit. I will
address these features later in this chapter.

The first time I contacted an insurance agent about purchasing a long-term care insurance policy, I was given a proposal which I thought too expensive and I did not purchase a policy. This was unfortunate. I was aware that anyone, at any age, may need long-term care services and I wanted protection from this risk. It took five more years before a different insurance agent helped me design a suitable long-term care insurance policy that met my goals and budget. Of course, when I purchased my policy I was five years older, so my premium, which is age-adjusted, was higher then it would have been five years earlier.

I encourage consumers to shop for insurance policies companies, and agents to get the coverage they need. I also suggest that you ask an insurance agent if he or she has any specialized training in long-term care insurance and senior issues. Long-term care insurance can be a confusing topic even for a trained insurance professional, but it is important that consumers understand the strengths and limitations of a policy before purchasing long-term care insurance.

I will try to make some of the features of long-term care insurance easier for you to understand. But first, let me give you an example of how long term care insurance can help to reduce the stress for a patient and his or her family when illness strikes.

The wife of an Alzheimer's patient who visited her husband every day, told me how difficult it had been to place her husband in a nursing home. She had wanted to keep him at home, but as his illness and confusion progressed, she realized that she could no longer provide proper care for him by herself. He was on the move at all hours of the day and night. Several times she had to search her neighborhood looking for her confused partner. Sometimes she found him. Other times he was brought home by a neighbor or the police. Over time, she became afraid for his safety. Part-time home care was ineffective, and twenty-four hour home care was financially out of reach. She realized that their best option was the Alzheimer's unit of a local nursing home.

It seemed to me that his wife had made a courageous and appropriate decision when she had her husband admitted to the nursing home. Yet she told me that her adult children, who lived out of town and had provided no hands-on caregiving for their father, questioned her decision. They would call and tell her, "Dad should come home. He's not that bad."

I just listened. As an investigator, it was not my job to comment on any family's personal business. But did they really think their dad should be home? Did they realize that their mother was exhausted? Did they know that their mother went to visit every day? Or were they simply worried that their mother was spending her life savings (which also could be thought of as her children's inheritance) to pay for her husband's nursing home care?

We can all learn a valuable lesson from stories like this. In the above case, a comprehensive long-term care insurance policy could have paid for care at the patient's home, in an assisted-living facility or in a nursing home. Regrettably, for those who already have serious health problems or will soon need long-term care services, it is usually too late to purchase a policy. Insurance companies have medical underwriting standards to keep the cost of long-term care insurance affordable. The premiums for a long-term care insurance policy will depend on variables such as your health status, the amount of coverage you purchase and your age (remember, you will never be younger than you are now).

Long-term care insurance allows you to customize your own plan by selecting when, where, how much, and what type of care that will be covered by the policy. The National Association of Insurance Commissioners (NAIC) has written "A Shopper's Guide to Long-term Insurance" to help consumers understand their long-term care insurance options. By law, this guide must be given to consumers by insurance companies or their agents, to help you better understand long-term care insurance and decide which, if any, policy fits your specific needs. "The Shopper's Guide to Long-term Care Insurance" asks the consumer the following questions. They are important considerations for anyone considering purchasing long-term care insurance..

Is Long-term Care Insurance Right for You?
You should NOT buy long-term care insurance if:

- You can't afford the premiums
- You have limited assets
- Your only source of income is a Social Security benefit or Supplemental Security Income (SSI)
- You often have trouble paying for utilities, food, medicine or other important needs

You should CONSIDER buying long-term care insurance if:

- You have significant assets and income
- You want to protect some of your assets and income
- You want to pay for your own care
- You want to stay independent of the support of others

Federally Tax-qualified Long-term Care Insurance Policies

A federally tax-qualified long-term care insurance policy, or a qualified policy, offers certain federal income tax advantages. For example, benefits paid by a qualified policy are generally not taxable as income. Also, you may be able to add premiums, subject to certain limitations, to your other medical expenses if you itemize deductions (the federal government also provides tax benefits for employers and self-employed individuals). If you elect to take out a policy, check with your tax advisor to find out if, and how much, you can deduct.

Guaranteed Renewal

Most long-term care policies sold today are guaranteed renewable. Therefore, the companies guarantee the consumer the chance to renew the policy. However, it does not mean that the insurer guarantees that the policyholder can renew at the same premium. The premium may go up over time as the insurance company pays more and larger claims. That is what happened to an eighty-one year-old woman who received an unexpected rate increase of 45 percent on her long-term care insurance policy. She was given two options in a letter from her insurer.

Option 1: Retain her current policy and accept the 45 percent increase in her premium, which would go from $182.79 to $265.05 per month.

Option 2: Select the contingent "non-forfeiture benefit," which is equal to all premiums paid, less any claims that have been paid by the insurance company. The non-forfeiture benefit is a sum of money which will be kept for her by the insurance company. This benefit can be used to pay future claims in accordance with the provisions listed on the insurance policy until the sum of money is exhausted.

     This elderly widow was put in a very difficult position by the dramatic rate increase. On one hand, she lost confidence in her insurance company and began considering the non-forfeiture benefit. On the other hand, as someone who had already suffered a severe financial loss paying for her husband's nursing home care before his death, she did not want to give up the protection offered by her policy. The third choice in this case was to purchase a long-term care policy from a highly rated insurance company with no history of rate increases. Unfortunately, after inquiry, this option, due to her health, age and finances, was not viable.

     It is important for consumers to give serious consideration to the third-party independent ratings of an insurance company *before* they purchase a guaranteed renewable insurance product, especially long-term care insurance. There are always many unknowns regarding the expected claim history for this relatively new type of insurance. Ask your insurance agent or insurer to provide you with the ratings of the insurance company from one or more of the following sources:

• A.M. Best Company, www.ambest.com

• Duff & Phelps, Inc., www.dcreo.com

- Fitch Investors Service, Inc, www.fitchibca.com
- Moody's Investor Service, Inc., www.moodys.com
- Standard and Poor's Insurance Rating Services, www.ratings.standardpoor.com
- Weiss Research, Inc., www.weissinc.com

Sharing the Risk

There are many steps you can take to design a long-term care insurance policy that fits your own budget, goals and needs while remaining financially viable. One way to reduce your premium is to share the risk with your insurer.

Elimination Period

The elimination period, sometimes called a deductible or waiting period, represents the number of days that you elect to personally pay for services before your policy activates. If you chose an elimination period of one hundred days, you pay a lower premium than if you were to choose an elimination period of fifty days. The self-insurance portion of your plan should take into consideration the amount of money you would be willing to pay before your long-term care insurance policy begins to pay benefits.

Although Americans should not rely on Medicare to pay for their long-term care, it is possible that Medicare might provide some limited coverage. For example, there is a chance that Medicare will pay for up to one hundred days of nursing home care when a patient meets their very strict guidelines. However, whether or not Medicare pays, a person who is confident that he or she could pay out-of-pocket for the first one hundred days of care at home, in an assisted-living facility or a nursing home can choose a one hundred day elimination period in order to reduce their long-term care insurance premium. A longer elimination period, since it allows the insurance company to share a greater portion of its risk, will most likely lower costs in the long term.

Daily Benefit

Long-term care insurance policies usually pay benefits by the day, week or month. Insurance companies let you choose the benefit amount. If a policy covers home care and assisted living, the benefit is usually calculated as a percentage of the nursing home benefit. It is important for consumers to know how much skilled nursing homes, assisted-living facilities and home health agencies charge for their services before they choose a benefit amount for their policy. These costs vary among different regions, therefore it is important to check the prices in the area where you think you might eventually need care. Doing so will allow you to accurately gauge the benefit amount you require to meet the potential costs of long-term care.

There is an opportunity for many Americans to self-insure at least part of the long-term care risk with money from a pension, Social Security or other source of income. This is an area that requires careful evaluation and an understanding of your own individual risk tolerance. For example, if the cost of nursing home care in a given area is $9,000 per month, a daily benefit of $300 per day would cover the full cost. A consumer who feels comfortable that he or she could contribute $3,000 per month from Social Security and other income if long-term care is needed could purchase a policy with a $200 per day benefit. Then, if nursing home care is eventually necessary, the insurer would pay $6,000 per month and the consumer would pay the rest as an out-of-pocket expense. As with other features of long-term care and most other types of insurance, you will find that you are asked to pay higher premiums for higher levels of coverage.

Maximum Benefit Limit

Most long-term care insurance policies limit the total amount of benefit they will pay over the term of the policy. This is often referred to as the "available pool of money." For example, if a consumer purchased a policy that covered $100 per day for three years (1,095 days), the total dollar value of the benefits this policy would pay out would be $109,500.

$$\$100 \times 1,095 \text{ (days)} = \$109,500.$$

A policy holder can usually spend their pool of money in any combination of home, assisted living or nursing home care within the terms of their policy. The maximum benefit is usually stated in years, for example, two, three, or five years. Some policies have no limit and they will pay for the lifetime of the policy holder. Of course, the longer the benefit period, the higher the premium.

Inflation Protection
Since long-term care insurance is usually considered a future benefit, inflation protection can be one of the most important features of a long-term care insurance policy. Keeping up with the rising costs of nursing homes and other long-term care services is important, because you may not need the benefits for many years. If the time comes when you do need long-term care, you want be sure that the daily benefits you purchased have increased in accordance with the inflated cost of care.

Although inflation protection increases the premium for long-term care insurance, it is often a worthwhile choice. For example, the daily benefit will double in fifteen years for a long-term care insurance policy with five percent compound inflation protection. This is an important feature to consider, since the actual cost of providing care in the future, which is subject to inflation, will undoubtedly be higher than it is today.

It is important for those who are considering the purchase of long-term care insurance to make certain that the policy is affordable and worth the cost. If done right the first time, you should not have to purchase more than one policy in your lifetime.

Partnership Programs

Some states (and I wish it were all states) have insurance programs that provide incentives for people to purchase long-term care insurance policies. These states, in the interest of protecting taxpayers from huge costs associated with providing for the elderly, form a partnership among a consumer, an insurer and the state Medicaid program. These plans require participants to purchase a certified long-term care insurance policy for the opportunity to protect their assets when they enroll in Medicaid. At present, there are four states participating with approved partnership programs. Three states, California, Connecticut and Indiana, use a "dollar for dollar" model, which provides that every dollar paid out by a certified insurer will be deducted from the resources counted toward Medicaid eligibility.

New York uses the "total assets" model, which requires that a participant obtain a certified insurance policy that covers three years of nursing home coverage and/or six years of home care, with each day of home care counting as a half day toward the three-year nursing home limit. If you buy a long-term care insurance policy under the New York State Partnership for Long-Term Care and you use your benefits according to the conditions of the program, you may apply for New York State Medicaid and still retain *all* your assets. There is no limit to the assets you may keep and still receive Medicaid Extended Coverage. However, your eligibility for Medicaid is based on your countable gross income. If determined eligible, you are required to contribute your income toward the cost of your care, in accordance with regular Medicaid rules.

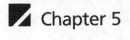 Chapter 5

Home Care

" 'Home' is any four walls that enclose the right person."
Helen Rowland, *Reflections of a Bachelor Girl* (1903)

Home care is a workable solution for many dependents and their families. Remember, patients do not need caregivers until they have some type of disability that keeps them from caring for themselves and most patients want to remain in their own home. Some patients are just lucky; they find a compassionate, honest and competent home aid. These patients have many quality years added to their lives. Others are not as fortunate—they become victims during their time of need. As we have seen, the abuse may be physical, financial, or both.

I have had the opportunity to meet thousands of patients who have some degree of home care in their own home. The majority of these patients needed some part-time assistance with daily living: help with recording medications, meal preparation, cleaning, bathing and dressing. Many patients received sophisticated treatments, such as oxygen and massage, at home with portable equipment. On the other hand, some of the patients that I have visited at their homes were confined to a hospital bed. They required continuous medical intervention from such equipment as ventilators and intravenous treatments.

I strongly suggest that you contact all of the available resources in your community to help you with the important decisions regarding home care. (Refer to the appendix of this book for the address and phone numbers of several reliable home care organizations.) Contact the geriatric division of your hospital, as well as religious organizations in your community, neighbors, friends and relatives who have experienced home care situations. Visit your local Department of Aging, local chapter of Alzheimer Disease and Related Disorder Association, as well as the home care agencies in your neighborhood.

The overwhelming majority of home care workers, whether Certified Home Health Aides, nurses, or therapists, are quality professionals who are dedicated to their patients. You need simply to protect yourself from the small minority that have a hidden agenda.

If you are in your later years, evaluate carefully your home care needs before illness strikes. You may benefit from the advice of an experienced health care professional such as a geriatric social worker or geriatric nurse when you entertain this decision. Remember that you want this arrangement to succeed, so don't short-change yourself. Appraise the responsibilities that your home care professional would have to perform. If you become dependent, or know someone who is, prepare a schedule which includes the type of professional assistance that you require, the number of hours necessary and the frequency of the shifts. This will be a beginning.

I suggest that before you hire any health professional, verify his or her license and have him or her fill out some type of application. I have included a sample application in the summary of this chapter.

Now make a detailed inventory of your home. Take a deep breath; help is on the way. Next, start removing any temptations such as cash, jewelry and valuables from harm's way. Keep a written record of where you have placed these articles. Arrange for income to be directly deposited into financial accounts to remove the opportunity for forgery or theft. As a friend or relative, you should prepare yourself to make unannounced visits. Complete the **Emergency Contact Information Sheet** that is included at the end of this book so that you have one source which contains vital information you may need if any emergency develops. Keep this worksheet in a safe, secure area.

Home care for older patients often requires a safety analysis of the home. Take the time to evaluate your environment. Contact the resource centers that are identified in the summary of this chapter and appendix of this book. Experience and research have taught us lessons on home safety. Take the time to do a thorough evaluation. An injury such as a fractured hip from a fall, could eliminate home care as an option. Start removing any hazards, make every effort to create a safe environment.

As we shall see, these basic precautions are not enough to prevent the tragedy of domestic violence and neglect as it affects the elderly everywhere.

All in the Family

Elder abuse can be a family affair. There are situations when an elder is the economic foundation of a household. As mounting expenses bankrupt a previously strong household, the quality of care offered to an elder can be affected by financial reality. Some patients become victims of their own family's greed and unskilled or negligent behavior. A defenseless patient can very easily become a hostage in his or her own home...that's what happened to Helen.

Four generations of the family had lived at 12 Maple Street. Helen, against all odds, had bought this four-bedroom colonial more than sixty years ago. In the old days, the house was filled with sounds of excitement and struggle, laughter and pain *and* song and conversation. Today, Helen is lying in a hospital bed in her living room all alone. There is no music, no talking, no care or attention. Her daughter is at work, her granddaughter is in the backyard sleeping and her two great-grandchildren are in school. The home mortgage was paid in full almost thirty years ago, so no rent is paid. Helen receives a pension check and social security every month. This money is controlled by her daughter. It is used for food and clothes for the daughter's family. Last year when Helen had her second stroke, she qualified for a home health aide.

Guess who the agency hired to attend to Helen? Her grand-daughter, who is still sleeping in the backyard. You would be sleeping too, if you took drugs and drank as much as Helen's granddaughter does. Normally, when private or government health insurance autho-rizes home care for a patient, they expect a family to protect, not take advantage of a patient. Without the monitoring that planning ensures, anything is possible in the shadowy homes that some of our less fortu-nate elderly are forced to occupy.

Quality elder care is extremely expensive but is worth every penny. There is no point in waiting: future costs will not be any less than they are now. Costs will increase, but the need cannot ethically be ignored.

We have to protect ourselves by consulting with legal, financial and medical professionals before a crisis develops. Take the time to fill out the **Emergency Contact Information Sheet**, located in the appendix. If you are a family or friend of an older person, help your older loved one fill it out. And remember to keep copies in a secure place.

Open House

The thick scar across the front of her neck was not the first thing I noticed about Maryanne. She was an elegant lady with short cropped brown hair, was well-dressed and perfectly polite. Maryanne appeared to blend well into the fabric of her wealthy suburban community.

Maryanne and her husband, Jack, had three empty bedrooms in their suburban home. Their three children had left the nest several years before. Now, Maryanne was concerned that her mother, Annie, who was terminally ill with breast cancer, should not return from the hospital to her apartment in the city. Jack and Maryanne converted the guest room on the first floor into a bedroom for Annie, complete with a hospital bed, IV and other medical equipment necessary to bring Annie into their home. They hired a contractor to install an atrium window so that Annie would have a view of the garden and be able to enjoy the serenity of their backyard.

Maryanne and Jack had a bad experience with domestic help and they had inventoried their valuables fifteen years ago, before they had hired their first cleaning service.

Maryanne called a neighbor for a reference on a live-in home health aide for their mother. Maryanne then checked other references before she invited Rosie to live with her from Monday through Friday in order to take care of her mom. Rosie was an experienced, compassionate human being and was able to provide adequate home care to Annie during the work week. Rosie became like a granddaughter to Annie.

Maryanne owned a prosperous real estate agency about fifteen minutes from her home. She would go home at least three times a day to spend time with her mother and feed her lunch. Maryanne had a special bond with her mom.

Every Friday at 5:00 P.M., Rosie's boyfriend, Ray, entered the circular driveway with the top of his glistening red convertible down. Rosie was always waiting at the front door. Like clockwork, on Monday at 9:00 A.M., Ray would drop Rosie back at Maryanne's house. This arrangement went on for more than two months.

Then suddenly on a Saturday night, Annie fell into a coma and was rushed to the hospital. The doctors and nurses told Maryanne that the prognosis for her mother was dim. She was unlikely to come out of the coma.

Maryanne called Rosie and told her the bad news. Maryanne set up camp at her mother's bedside, determined to be at her side if she should awaken. For three days, Maryanne slept in a chair next to her mom at the hospital.

At 7:00 A.M. on Tuesday, Annie died.

Maryanne felt an empty feeling in her stomach. She was in a daze as she drove home on familiar streets with the vivid memory of Annie's death etched in her mind.

Because of her shock and grief, Maryanne did not notice the familiar red convertible, Ray's car—the one he used to drive Rosie to and from work. Maryanne walked into her house as it was being burglarized by Ray and his friend Lou. Ray panicked and took Maryanne upstairs and tied her to a chair. Then he wrapped a rope around her mouth to keep her from screaming. Ray continued to clean out the house. When he was done, he decided to kill Maryanne since she could identify him. He cut her throat and left her to die. After Ray and Lou left, Maryanne had the strength to dial 911. The police arrived at the house within minutes, with an ambulance behind them.

In short order, the police sent out an All Points Bulletin (APB). Within an hour, Ray and Lou were arrested.

Maryanne was taken to the very hospital that her mother had died in earlier that morning. Maryanne recovered with multiple stitches placed in her neck. She was unable to attend her own mother's funeral.

Maryanne consoled herself with the thought that there could have been two funerals that day: mother and daughter. She thought often, since that day, how close she came to joining her mother in death.

This could have been prevented:
- No matter how difficult, try not to let strangers know when you are not going to be home.
- When home care employees are no longer needed, have them leave in your presence. Change the locks if they had any access to an entry key or combination lock.
- If possible, install an alarm system which can be activated when you leave the premises. Many alarms have a portable remote control unit which can be carried in a pocket or purse and which can

be activated to call the police with just a touch. These remote units are sometimes called panic buttons and they are an inexpensive component of home security systems.

An Ounce of Prevention

Max was the last person you would expect to have senile dementia, the medical term used to describe one of the memory afflictions that may strike the elderly. Max ran his hardware business without a cash register for forty years. He would look at the items that his customer purchased and instantly figure the total out in his head. His credit line was handled in the same way. If a person told him he or she would pay later, he never forgot what you bought and what you owed. If the IRS did not insist that he use a register and keep his books and records, Max would never have used a paper document to run his business. Even after his memory loss began, Max still maintained a surprising memory for numbers.

Three years after his wife Ida died, Max was found by the police wandering two miles from his home in a state of confusion. Gail Gordon, the police officer in the case, was only twenty-six-years-old, but she handled Max like a veteran. First thing, she asked Max to sit on a bench. He was sobbing hysterically. She began to reassure him that everything was going to be all right. Fortunately for Max, Officer Gordon found Max's son's business card in Max's wallet as she was placing him in an ambulance. Mark was waiting for his father at the hospital. At ninety-one, Max was still in good physical health and he was usually alert or lucid. As he recovered, Max stated repeatedly that he did not want to go to a nursing home. He felt strongly about remaining in his own home.

Mark took out an advertisement in the local paper and hired the first person he interviewed. The "companion" he hired lived near Max.

Tom, a middle-aged home health aide, claimed to have extensive experience. Tom had spent ten years working as an orderly at the community nursing home and his recommendation stated that he was great with the patients. Observers noted that he talked and listened to his patients and they all appreciated his unusual cooking skills. Tom would visit Max twice a day for two three-hour shifts. Each tour, Tom would prepare a meal for Max and remind him to take his medications. Max would spend the weekends with his son and daughter-in-law. This arrangement went on for three months. Then, suddenly, Tom told Mark he was leaving the state and moving to Florida.

This time Mark contacted the a licensed home care agency and arranged for a replacement. Mark decided that before he hired a new aide, he had better place his father's valuables and cash in a safe, or in a safety deposit box.

It was too late. Max's things had been cleaned out by Tom! Mark couldn't find his father's coin collection, antique watches, or his mother's jewelry. There was no cash or checks anywhere in the apartment. Max could not provide any clue to the missing items and Tom was long gone. It was later learned that Tom had a criminal record with three convictions for petty larceny. He had learned to cook in jail.

Don't become a VICTIM; take the following steps:
- Inventory your belongings before you allow a stranger into your house.
- Safeguard all valuables in a safe deposit box or some type of protected area.
- Limit the access of any home care personnel to a defined patient area.
- Request the home care agency to notify you if the employee they have sent you has a criminal history. Most employers ask for this information on their application. Granted, people lie on their applications, but this false statement can be useful for prosecution in a court of law.

"We Trusted Her"

Dorothy's ninetieth birthday was celebrated in her retirement home located on a peaceful canal in northern Florida. Dorothy had plenty of visitors from the north during the cold winter months and her family and friends would take turns using the two spacious guest rooms. The live-in home health aide, Susan, would prepare the meals and rooms for the visitors and her client, Dorothy. However, her milestone birthday was the first time in five years that her three adult children and their families were together in the same room.

Chilled shrimp and many other appetizers were served on the patio which gave a picturesque view of the spacious canal. Luxury cabin cruisers routinely passed the birthday celebration and gave a horn blast and cheer. Two dolphins swam past the dock as if they were part of the entertainment. It was a wonderful day to be ninety.

This celebration was the first time that John had met his fiancee Mary's family and he was impressed. John was a CPA, CFE and a senior forensic accountant with a law firm in Washington, D.C. John casually asked his future father-in-law, Michael, how much does a party like this cost in Florida? Michael's reply, that Dorothy's finances were handled by the home health aide, surprised John.

Michael explained that he had accepted responsibility for his mother's finances about ten years ago. He used electronic banking to balance his mother's account. All of her income was direct deposited electronically into a money management account which was held jointly in both Dorothy's and Michael's names. Susan was given a debit type of credit card that was linked directly to the joint account.

Susan was allowed to use this card to shop for food, clothes and other items for Dorothy. Michael would routinely review the balance in the account, but he never asked for any back-up records from Susan. John hesitated about interfering in Dorothy's business. He just listened.

Upon hearing John's question, Michael realized that he had not really checked his mother's finances for at least two years. John volunteered to help Michael if he wanted to check the records after the party.

The preliminary review of the debit card expenses concerned John, especially since the records were limited to the monthly statements and there were no individual charge receipts. John suggested that Michael verify the delivery of a few of the big ticket items, such as the television and VCR.

Michael called the customer service department of the electronics store and he was told that the TV and VCR were delivered to Susan's daughter who lived out of state. This was just the tip of the iceberg, more than half of the items charged to Dorothy's account were for Susan.

Susan cried hysterically when she confessed to her fraud. She had no history of fraud and she claimed that she had never stolen anything before. Susan claimed that when she discovered that no one was checking Dorothy's financial records, she started cheating a little at a time. She found that it was so easy to steal that she simply could not resist the temptation. She confessed that she didn't have the ability to return the stolen goods. Michael couldn't resist the need to let this otherwise kind aide go.

This fraud could have been prevented by taking the following steps:
- Whenever possible do not give a home care worker access to a patient's finances—distribute funds on an as needed basis.
- Obtain detailed receipts for any items that are purchased on your behalf by paid assistants.
- Independently verify that all purchases are legitimate and, if an item is delivered, request the invoice with an address of delivery.
- Maintain your own version of a monthly budget, in order to identify any unusual expenses.

Summary: A Six-Step Guide to Home Care

Step 1: Prepare the Home

- **Hazards:** locate and remove small step-stools, loose rugs, runners, mats, electrical cords, telephone lines. The objective is to create a safe environment for an elder patient with some loss of hearing and sight. Be thorough! An elder patient is very fragile, and a fall can cause a serious injury.

- **Night Light and Lighting:** Install a night light that will provide a clear path for a patient to locate the bathroom at night. In addition, install brighter lights in the home that will be adequate for the elder to see clearly in the evening.
- **Clocks:** Place large face clocks throughout the home to assist the patient with time and day orientation.
- **The Bedroom:** Provide sturdy furniture or guardrails to assist the patient to safely enter and exit his or her bed.
- **Everything on One Level:** Patient safety may require that the bathroom, kitchen and bedroom all be on one level to avoid the potential injury of a fall on the stairs. Safeguard all stairways with doors that can easily be closed.
- **Smoke Detectors:** Install smoke detectors throughout the home, especially in the kitchen. Also, consider carbon-monoxide detectors. Older people confined to the home need to be assured of pure air within it.
- **Burglar Alarms:** A burglar alarm system can add to the safety of an elder. Many of these include a "medical alert" feature, which can be activated with a remote option. The touch of a button can bring police and EMS workers to the side of a needy senior.
- **Modifications:** Handles and faucets should be modified for easier use by elder patients, especially for those with arthritis. Special medicine bottles that are easy to open are also available.
- **Phones:** Phones should be accessible throughout the home so that emergency calls can easily be made. A phone should be placed conveniently by the bed for emergency use. Remember to install all telephone cords in a safe manner. Volume control phones are designed to assist clients with hearing losses. Speaker phones relieve a patient of the burden of holding a phone.
- **Slippery Floors:** Bathrooms and stairs, especially, must be modified to prevent injuries.
- **Bathrooms:** Must be modified or possibly remodeled to accom-

modate safety features such as handrails, grab-bars, non-slip floors, or mats in tubs and shower stalls. This is extremely important for people who use wheelchairs or walkers.

- **Radios, Remote Control Televisions and Reading Lights in the Bedroom:** Design entertainment centers to allow the elder patient convenience with minimal exposure to injury. Avoid distances and sharp corners.

- **Elder Care Organizations:** Many advocate organizations can provide additional guidance and resources for safeguarding an elder patient's home environment. The following organizations (addresses and phone numbers are included in the appendix section) are a few of the many organizations that can assist you with home care: the Department of Aging, the American Association of Retired Persons (AARP), the Alzheimer Association and the Children of Aging Parents.

Step 2: Safeguard Valuable Personal and Financial Possessions

- **Remove Temptation:** All cash should be placed in a bank or other type of financial institution. Jewelry, bankbooks, credit cards, checkbooks, checks and collector's items should be placed in protected locations, such as hidden safes or bank safe deposit boxes.

- **Direct Deposit:** Social Security checks, pension and investment checks should be directly deposited into accounts to prevent theft and forgery.

- **Alcohol and Expired Medications:** These should be removed in order to prevent accidental overdose by patient or abuse by home care workers.

- **Cars and Vehicles:** Home care workers should not have access to cars, trucks, boats, or other vehicles that are owned by the patient, or the patient's family.

Step 3: Obtain and Install Medical Equipment

Elder patients who are discharged from hospitals or nursing homes to their home(s) may require special medical equipment. Portable medical equipment, such as respirators, ventilators and other services, are often installed in the home. A patient may require a hospital bed, wheelchair, or a commode. Many companies rent this equipment; rental of equipment is frequently covered by health insurance and Medicare. However, I suggest that you only accept the equipment that you need: I have been in the homes of elder patients who were tricked into renting equipment that they did not want or use. This excess equipment can become a safety hazard and add enormously to the personal cost of health care. I have met many elders who complain that a health care provider would not reclaim unnecessary equipment. I strongly recommend that if this happens to you or your caregiver, call the Attorney General's Office in your state (the addresses and phone numbers are included in the appendix).

Step 4: Selecting the Home Care Worker

- **Network:** Contact friends, relatives, clergy, community organizations and especially senior advocates for referrals.
- **Conduct Telephone Screening:** Screen applicants during telephone interviews as a method of reducing the stress of multiple face-to-face interviews. Describe in a professional manner the full details of the duties and obligations of the home care worker. Give the location of your neighborhood but do *not* immediately give your address. Discuss salary, get the names and addresses of references and prior clients. Also obtain the license or certification numbers of the candidate. Verify all of the furnished information *before* you conduct a face-to-face interview. Conclude the telephone interview by obtaining the phone number of the candidate to arrange for a potential in-person interview.
- **Interview Home Care Candidates with Another Person:** If at all possible, conduct your interviews with another person present, possibly one of your relatives or a friend. You will have the benefit of a second opinion and you will send a message: this patient and those around the patient are attentive, involved and aware.

- **Employment Application:** Have employees furnish you with applications which include: name, address, phone number, social security number, driver's license number, as well as car registration number. Also, review professional licenses and verify their status. Finally, obtain a detailed employment history (you may use the sample application located in Step 5).
- **Discuss the Possibility of Theft:** This discussion can be helpful to the employee as well as the patient. Elder patients may, at times, become disoriented and accuse employees of stealing items that they, themselves, have misplaced. The discussion of theft should include a survey of the home care environment and any limitations regarding access. For example, in a two-level home in which the bedridden patient is living downstairs, the second floor should be off limits.
- **Conduct Your Own Background Checks:** Request that any prospective employee agree to a criminal background check. This can be part of your application, which should include a general release form which gives you permission from the applicant to obtain information to verify the accuracy of their application. Your attorney should be in a position to assist you to design an application that meets the specific requirements of your state. (I have provided a sample copy in Step 5).
- **Consider Several Applicants and Agencies:** Attempt to interview several referred candidates for several reasons, including having a choice and having alternates in the event of a crisis.
- **Establish a Clear Payment Schedule and Detail Responsibilities:** Never ask home care workers to perform services for which they are not licensed. For example, do not ask personal care aides to give injections of medicine, most are not authorized to administer them under your state law. Such an act constitutes a crime and may subject you to criminal prosecution.
- **Ensure Compatibility:** Make sure that the home care worker is compatible with the patient. There is no reason for any homebound patient to be forced into receiving care from an employee that he or she fears or dislikes.

Step 5:

Employment Application

Name _____

Professional Degrees and Certificates _____

License Number _____

Date of Graduation _____

Expiration Date

Employment History:

Employer _____

Address/Phone Number _____

Dates of Employment _____

Reason for Leaving _____

_____

_____

Personal References:

Name _____

Address/Phone Number _____

Relationship _____

Name _____

Address/Phone Number _____

Relationship _____

Criminal History:

Have you ever been convicted of a crime?   Yes   No

If yes, please provide all details (which crime, when, have you been in prison?) _____

_____

Authorization to Conduct a Verification and Background Investigation:

I, _____, state that all of the information stated in this employment application is true, to the best of my knowledge. I authorize my prospective employer permission to verify all of the information that I furnished on this application.

Signature _____

Step 6: Respite Care

The home care patient and family most often benefit from social contact outside of the home. Alert and ambulatory elder patients should participate in senior citizen activities within their communities if they intend to slow declining physical and mental fitness. One senior citizen, Mary, became severely disabled and required a walker or wheelchair to ambulate. This determined and spirited senior could not walk more than fifteen feet before she had to stop and catch her breath. Still, Mary refused to be isolated. She attended her senior activities every day, playing cards and eating with her friends.

In contrast, I remember vividly a bedridden homebound patient who was living with his family. This patient, Paul, received love and attention from his daughter Ellen, but he had very little contact with the outside world. My interview with Paul verified that he had adequately received all of the services that were billed by the many health providers who provided home care. During my visit, Paul's daughter stood by the side of his hospital bed, her arm braced against the bedrail as she affectionately held her father's hand. Ellen told me that her father did not talk anymore. I looked at Paul, as he lay in his bed and he looked back at me.

"Hello, Paul. My name is Tom. I am here to ask a few questions about some of the medical services that you receive."

"*How old are you?*" said Paul.

I was told by the family that Paul had not talked to anyone for over six months. Paul asked me about my children and how long I had worked as an investigator. I did not expect Paul to answer my questions and I was surprised. His daughter was shocked, to say the least.

I could not, due to the constraints of my career, conduct an interview in the presence of a patient without explaining the purpose of my visit. The official aspect of my job is not to socialize. Although I am not an expert in patient care, I am convinced that homebound patients and their caregivers benefit from social contact. All that I had to do was to treat Paul as a responsible, intelligent human being and he broke briefly out of his shell.

Today, there are many services available to homebound patients and families. For example:

- **Adult Daycare Centers:** There are many levels of adult daycare centers, including those affiliated with hospitals and nursing homes which provide extensive medical care. These centers often provide meals and activities and perhaps more importantly, the companionship of new friends.

- **Senior Centers:** These centers offer activities and social contact within a community for self-sufficient senior citizens. These organizations often provide recreational activity and education for their members as well.

- **Clergy:** Many religious denominations provide home visits to homebound patients.

- **Meals-On-Wheels:** This service provides homebound patients with nutritious meals at low cost. Often this service is provided by volunteers in the community.

- **Hospitals:** Many hospitals have geriatric divisions which can assist patients in locating valuable resources.

- **Colleges or Universities:** Educational institutions often have a gerontology, sociology, medical school, or another related program that can assist a patient or family locate assistance.

- **Department of Aging:** Contact your local department of aging and senior citizen offices to locate other social services that are available in your community.

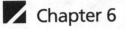 Chapter 6

Assisted-living Facilities

In the opinion of many working in the elder care sector, assisted-living residences will become a twenty-first century growth industry for corporate America. No longer will these facilities be exclusively operated by "mom and pop" types of small businesses. Major hotel chains and national corporations are now actively establishing themselves in the nursing home and assisted-living industry. Skilled nursing facilities (see Chapter 7) participate in a regulated industry, where there are trained health care personnel and full time nursing supervision. The fastest growing segment of the American population are those eighty-five years or older. There were 3.3 million members of this cohort in 1990 and the expectation is that their members will reach almost six million by the year 2010 and fifteen million by 2050.

Assisted-living residences can provide a comfortable living environment for a client (not patient), at significantly less expense than a nursing home. However, assisted-living residences are *not* nursing homes. Many assisted-living residences do not participate in any government third party payment programs, such as Medicare or Medicaid. Therefore, they are not regulated by these programs and the majority of their clients are private payers. This type of residence provides meals, social activities, educational programs, transportation and other pro-

grams to its customers. In addition, many of these residences assist their
clients with personal care and medications. Staff members might record
their clients' medications or remind them when they should take their
prescriptions, but they are limited by each state in the personal care
that they are allowed to provide.

An assisted-living residence is a general term that includes residential non-medical facilities. These residences may be known in your
community by some of the following names: "custodial care facility,"
"rest home," "board and care home," "adult home," or "senior residence," and the list goes on. The assisted-living residence usually fur-
nishes a client with an admission agreement or contract, much like a
lease on an apartment. This contract, like most other contracts, should
be reviewed by an attorney—not the facility's attorney, *your* attorney. A
caveat to always keep in mind: *this is not a highly regulated industry, therefore, the consumer must always be on guard*.

Before you enter into an agreement, take the following steps:
- **Contact the Office of Aging:** Find out if the assisted-living residence is known to them and request a list of others in the vicin-
  ity so that you can have a choice.
- **Speak With Doctors:** Ask your doctor if he or she would recommend home aides or make house calls at the residence.
- **Visit Without Warning:** Make unannounced visits at different times
  of the day. Do the residents appear content? Are the meals appetiz-
  ing? Is the staff friendly and pleasant? Is the residence clean? Are there
  any unpleasant odors? Are there activities? If possible, eat a meal there.
- **Contact the Minister of Your Chosen Faith:** Determine what,
  if any, services they provide to the facility's residents. Ask for a recommendation of a social service.
- **Observe the Resident Clients:** Determine if the resident population is compatible to senior citizens.
- **Enumerate the Available Services:** Check personal care services such as hairstyling and barbers available, and at what costs.

- **Calender of Events:** Review the list of upcoming activities, if one exists.
- **Obtain and Review Available Information:** Review all brochures and admission agreements including all fee schedules. Review information with your attorney if you would seriously consider moving into the facility.
- **Determine Resident Occupancy:** Determine whether there are single rooms available and what other living arrangements are available.
- **Determine the Refund Policy:** In the event you voluntarily move, or if you require a different level of care determine if you can receive a refund.
- **Find Out:** The hospital, doctor and ambulance that is used in case of an emergency.
- **Discover Emergency Procedure:** Find out what the emergency policy of the residence is and the notification procedure: next of kin, etc.
- **Fill out an Emergency Contact Information Sheet:** The Emergency Contact Information Sheet in the back of this book will have most of the vital information that you or your family will need in cases of an emergency.

My Way

One case in particular exemplifies clear and rational decision-making on the part of a prepared senior citizen. Mary, a widow with three married children, was getting a little tired of maintaining her four bedroom colonial. At the age of seventy-six, she decided to accept her daughter Amy's invitation and move into her guest room. Within three months, Mary sold the house and invested her profits in income-producing tax-free municipal bonds to supplement her pension and social security. Mary had a will which divided her estate equally among her three children and she had completed a comprehensive personal history.

However, Mary, who had been living alone for ten years since her husband Jim died, did not adjust well to living with her daughter. With three teenage children, the hectic pace at Amy's house was a bit of a culture shock to Mary. The daily blast of rock music drowned the classical symphonies that played in Mary's bedroom.

Mary frequently visited her friend Louise at the Golden Gable Senior Hotel. The residence was located a short distance from the heart of the town where her daughter lived. This assisted-living residence had a one hundred percent senior citizen population. Mary was greeted by several of the residents who had befriended her. Mary and Louise had lunch in the dining room, during which Mary had a serious discussion with Louise about the living arrangements at the Golden Gables. Mary found that there were no hidden costs and that she could afford the monthly rent without dipping into her savings. Just to be on the safe side, Mary staggered her visits to Louise and came at different hours. Eventually, she met the administrator and agreed to be placed on the waiting list.

At first, Mary was reluctant to tell Amy of her decision; she was concerned that Amy would feel insulted or hurt. Amy was surprised, but pleased at her mother's choice since she would still be in their community. In addition, Amy was familiar with the reputation of the Golden Gable Senior Hotel—well known and respected in the community.

The Golden Gable Senior Hotel sent Mary a contract which was reviewed with her children and her attorney *before* she signed it. Mary kept her own doctor. If there was an emergency, she would be transferred to the hospital of her choice. Mary selected The Good Samaritan Hospital with which her doctors had been affiliated for years.

Mary has been a resident at the Golden Gable Senior Hotel for about three years now. Even though her friend Louise has been transferred to a nursing home, Mary has many new friends and refers to her room as her home. For the first time since her husband died, she feels at peace.

The Web We Weave

The rise and fall of "Teresa's Assisted-living Residential Empire" illustrates well why elder care consumers have to be careful. Teresa, a single parent with three children, had a plan. She bought a deteriorating assisted-living residence that was two steps away from total collapse. The old hotel looked like a haunted house at an amusement park and the disheveled residents looked like forgotten prisoners of war. This residence, ironically named "The Senior Palace," had an occupancy capacity of sixty residents but had a current census of only twenty-six abandoned elderly citizens.

Teresa bought "The Senior Palace" at a bargain price. Real estate agents thought she was going to tear down the building and sell the land to developers. However, Teresa had a plan. Within two months of her purchase, all sixty beds were occupied.

The thirty-four recent arrivals at "The Senior Palace" all came from the same place, the state psychiatric center. Teresa had changed the nature of the population of her adult home from a geriatric to a psychiatric one. Teresa worked day and night to keep the costs down and the occupancy at capacity. In one year she had almost paid the full balance of her private mortgage and had tripled her savings. Teresa then went shopping and bought another assisted-living residence. She repeated her success. Within five years, she had purchased four more residences and every one of them was at 100% capacity. Teresa utilized the formula of accepting psychiatric patients to fill any void in her occupancy rate.

Teresa expanded her real-estate empire to include private residences that she bought at foreclosure auctions. She had devised a plan to increase her residential occupancy higher than the legal limit. She would evaluate her clients and hide the overflow of residents by secretly transferring them to residential communities.

Teresa bought a Cape Cod-style home with a brick driveway and walkway in a secluded section of a working-class neighborhood.

She hired Jean, a welfare mother with two young children and a live-in boyfriend, to monitor up to six residents from Teresa's assisted-living empire. She let Jean and her family live full-time and rent-free in this house. Jean received all of her food, plus a cash stipend, each month. Teresa screened her residents in order to find older female clients with no family contacts. These clients wouldn't wander about the neighborhood and draw complaints from the community. This profit-making scheme worked for many years until one of the residents died.

Betsy was an eighty-six-year-old woman who had long since lost contact with her family. They thought she was still a resident at the Senior Palace. Instead, Betsy was watching television at a private home supervised by Jean. One particular Wednesday, Betsy was eating a peanut butter sandwich on day-old bread. Betsy's first bite caught in her throat. She started choking and gasping for air. Jean, the completely untrained "supervisor," watched in horror as Betsy fell to the kitchen floor. Jean did not call the police or an ambulance, since they might notify the welfare office. Instead, she moved the five other residents who were present back to the living room.

Then she called Teresa in a panic, telling her that Betsy was dead. Teresa rushed right over, fearing most of all that her assisted-living empire was teetering on the verge of collapse. She could not let that happen. She would not let that happen.

Arriving at the home twenty minutes later, Teresa tried to assure everyone that things were fine. She helped Jean move Betsy's body into a bedroom; then waited for darkness. When the sun went down and the street was dark and quiet, Teresa and Jean propped Betsy between them and, with her arms on each of their shoulders, they walked her out to the station wagon and placed her in the back seat. They followed the same procedure in reverse at the "Senior Palace" as they placed Betsy in a bed. Teresa then called her "house doctor" who came right over.

He pronounced Betsy dead and attributed it to natural causes.

This can be prevented by taking the following steps:
- Visit an assisted-living residence and ask to meet some of the guests. Around meal time is a good time to come, since most of the clients will be in the dining area. How satisfied are the residents? Take some of them aside, and find out the real story.
- Make unannounced visits and phone calls.
- Pay very close attention when a change of ownership takes place at any facility that houses and cares for someone you know.
- When suspicions of fraud arise, call the authorities immediately.

The End of the Line

Social isolation and family neglect are often the unpreventible and unenviable results of a long and active life; however, it is within our powers to ensure that each senior member of our families and communities get the dignity in care that each so intensely deserves.

Mandy had owned the Bayview Residence for almost thirty years and was planning for her own retirement in the next three years. At sixty-one, Mandy was in fairly good health except for her chronic obesity and expected hip replacement. Mandy's assisted living residence was situated on waterfront property with a breathtaking view of Lake Ontario. The Bayview Residence had been declared a historical landmark by the county. Mandy was very careful when she converted this abandoned hotel into a senior residence, preserving the lavish decor to comply with the property's upgraded building codes. In order to maintain expenses, the Bayview Residence did not accept any government subsidized residents—all of its clients paid higher private rates.

One of the resident's new clients, Bernadette, had been an extremely independent woman until the time that she was hospitalized for heart disease. Bernadette had been living in a one-room apartment for forty years and had been employed as an office manager at Northern State Psychiatric Center for almost fifty years, until she was forced to retire at the age of sixty-eight. Bernadette had been a patient at that psychiatric center herself. Bernadette's mother had died at her birth; she had had a torturous childhood during which her father blamed Bernadette for her mother's death. She had attempted suicide at age fifteen by jumping in front of a train; this caused her left leg to be amputated. After her recovery, she remained at the psychiatric hospital where she worked until her retirement.

Bernadette had low self-esteem and resigned herself to live the life of a hermit. She had worked every day, never even took a vacation or sick day and lived in a meager apartment with only the necessities to maintain her life. She ate most of her meals at the hospital dining room and took no visitors. Bernadette did, however, save her money. Every two weeks, when she was paid, seventy percent of her paycheck went into her credit union account. On top of that, fifty-years of employment as a state worker entitled her to a large pension, life insurance and a high social security income.

When the discharge planner at the hospital told Bernadette that she needed to transfer to an assisted-living residence within three weeks, Bernadette took a room with a water view at the Bayview Residence. A few days later, Mandy started asking Bernadette personal questions and discovered that Bernadette had no known relatives or friends. Mandy convinced Bernadette that she had to have a will. Mandy's lawyer was at the Bayview Residence the next day and the will, naming Mandy the sole beneficiary of Bernadette's estate and giving her power of attorney, was signed within a week.

Bernadette didn't like the other residents and became even more reclusive. She rarely left her room and never cleaned the decubitus ulcer that had developed on her left leg. No one suggested doing it for her. Mandy started closing her door because the other residents complained about the odor (from her decaying leg) which emanated from the room. She refused to transfer Bernadette to a hospital even though her staff complained that she needed hospital care. It wasn't until Mandy left the Bayview Residence for a luncheon at the country club that one of her employees, noticing Bernadette's leg, boldly called an ambulance to transfer Bernadette to St. Mary's Hospital emergency room.

Mandy, in an extreme panic, arrived at the emergency room two hours later. She immediately went to the admitting clerk to give her version of Bernadette's medical and personal history. She told the clerk and the nurse supervisor that Bernadette had given her (Mandy) a power of attorney, which gave her the right to act for Bernadette, in all matters   concerning her hospitalization. Mandy never mentioned that she was also beneficiary of Bernadette's will.

Mandy went on to tell the clerk and nurse how sad she was that "her friend" had terminal cancer. Two days later, Bernadette died in the hospital. Based on the hospital record, the doctor listed the cause of death as cancer.

However, Bernadette did not have cancer; she had died from neglect and greed.

Bernadette's untimely death could have been prevented:

- Community officers need to be persuaded to provide regular inspection of homes by social workers.
- If Bernadette had made a will naming a charity as the beneficiary, she would have removed the financial incentive for Mandy to keep her imprisoned in her room. She should have made the will long before hospitalization forced her into a dependent living arrangement.
- Bernadette should have pre-selected a residence long before the crisis came. Any senior living without the benefit of family assistance needs to make visits to area assisted-living residences in order to evaluate the potential care that he or she may soon be in need of.

Bernadette's case is also a prime example of how important volunteers are in institutions for the elderly. Social contact, however brief, is essential to emotional and physical health.

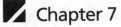 **Chapter 7**

Nursing Homes

During my almost twenty years as an investigator, I have toured a great many excellent nursing homes. I have also been in some terrifying ones. The first time that you visit a nursing home, you may be apprehensive about the condition of some of the patients. Remember that the patients sitting in the hallways near the nurses' station, the patients slowly walking to the activities room, or the invisible patients who are confined to beds or psychiatric wards did not choose to be placed in a nursing home. I don't know of any patient who wanted to be in a nursing home or wanted to rely on the assistance of a stranger.

And what has happened to bring you to the front door of a nursing home? I know of a thousand different reasons. You are here to see a dying relative, or, perhaps, to see yourself as you will appear one day. I know that there is pain and fear of the unknown. You have been encouraged to use every resource available to assist you in planning for the last leg of your life's journey. You want to make the best choice the first time.

The United States Department of Health and Human Services has written a helpful brochure titled "Guide to Choosing a Nursing Home," available to you upon request. The reality is that when it comes to choosing a nursing home, there may be very limited choices since the supply of nursing homes in your geographic area is likely to be decreasing as the population ages. If your choice is limited, there is no reason to panic. First, resolve not to settle for an inferior environment. Second, extend your search to a wider area until you find a compatible home. Finally, ask early to be placed on a waiting list for nursing homes that you find desirable.

A skilled nursing facility, which in this chapter is also referred to as a "nursing home," provides a high level of medical care and full-time nursing supervision. A nursing home can provide two types of services: short-term for rehabilitation purposes and long-term custodial care. Short-term rehabilitative care may be provided to a patient who is discharged from a hospital and is transferred to a nursing home for rehabilitation. The expectation is that he or she will be transferred to his or her home or to another, lower-level facility. This type of rehabilitation is often partially covered by insurance, including Medicare. The insurance coverage has limitations and each patient's coverage is evaluated individually.

Long-term custodial care is usually not covered by traditional insurance, including Medicare. At the point that a patient is a candidate for a nursing home, rushed decisions have to be made and usually one finds that there are not very many options available for payment. I suggest that you explore your individual situation with your attorney when he or she reviews your admission agreement. In addition, review the chapters on finance and legal issues in this book.

Nursing homes are inspected by regulatory agencies to ensure that they provide safe and healthy environments for the patients, staff and visitors. However, there is a tremendous difference between a well-run nursing home and the minimum standard. The inspection agencies, whether private or government, usually issue reports based upon the results of their routine inspections. Contact your state department of aging and ask for the number of the regulatory agency that certifies nursing homes in your state.

A Guide to the Nursing Home

The research that you conduct when you search for the best nursing home is always worth the effort. The following guide will assist you in your search for a compatible nursing home:

Step 1: Preliminaries

- **Referrals:** Ask for recommendations from friends, relatives, clergy, doctors, nurses and health professionals. Compile a list of these referrals and begin your search with the most frequently recommended facilities.
- **Location:** While location is often the most important factor in choosing a home to patients, families and friends who plan to visit patients, the nursing home needs to be accessible to public transportation, as well as having sufficient parking for visitors with cars. The grounds and surrounding areas should be well kept and serene for the patients who are mobile. Patients who are confused or incompetent should have regular visitors to act as advocates, since they cannot speak up for themselves. Frequent visitors send a message to the nursing home staff that somebody is monitoring the situation.
- **Inspection Reports:** Review all available inspection reports before and after you choose a nursing home. These reports are on file at applicable state, county and city agencies.
- **Visitors:** Are there many visitors with the patients? If there is a visitor's sign-in book, notice the number of visitors by each date. A good nursing home encourages visitors through out-reach to volunteer organizations.
- **"Guide to Choosing a Nursing Home":** Contact your congressional representative and request a copy of the government "Guide to Choosing a Nursing Home."
- **Contact the Office of Aging:** Find out if the nursing home that you have visited is known to state agencies and ask for a list of facilities in your geographic area.

- **Doctor Recommendation:** Contact your doctor for a recommendation. Find out if the doctor makes house calls to the facility. If not, find out what doctors are available to patients on a daily, weekly and emergency basis.
- **Unannounced Visits:** Make unannounced visits at different times of the day. Do the patients appear content? Are they clean? Is the staff friendly and pleasant? Is the facility clean? Are there any unpleasant odors? Are there social activities? Does the staff respond quickly to patients who need attention?
- **Admission Agreement:** Obtain and review the admission agreement, as well as all of the brochures and fee schedules. The admission agreement, which is a legal contract, should be seen by your entire family and attorney. *Make certain that you fully comprehend all of your legal and financial obligations.* Remember that you can request changes in your agreement *before* you sign it. For example, if you anticipate that you or your loved one may transfer to another nursing home when a bed becomes available, then you need to consider negotiating a waiver of the refund policy.
- **Clergy:** Contact the ministry of your chosen faith to determine what religious services are available to the patients at the nursing facility. Does a minister, priest, or rabbi visit the facility and patients on a regular basis? Are there scheduled religious services on-site?
- **Diet:** If the patient requires a special diet, such as vegetarian, no-salt or kosher, determine whether the nursing home can comply with your requests.
- **Roommates:** What is the policy at the nursing home regarding roommates? Does the home make an effort to match compatible patients? How many patients are in a room? How difficult is it to change rooms?
- **Activities:** Review the activities schedule and look for stimulating services for your individual needs. Are there social as well as physical activities?

- **Hospital:** Ask the admission representative for the names of the hospital, doctors and ambulance affiliated with the nursing home, in case of a medical emergency. Is the hospital nearby?
- **Emergency Procedure:** Find out what the emergency policy and notification procedure is at the nursing home.
- **Emergency Contact Information Sheet:** Complete the Emergency Contact Information Sheet in the back of this book. This vital information will assist both you and your family in the event of an emergency.
- **Patients:** Ask the admission representative for a tour of the facility. Talk to patients to find out about their opinion of the nursing home. Also, speak with the staff for their opinions. If possible, tour at meal times and have a sample meal.
- **Physical Restraints:** Find out the home's policy regarding physical restraints, to ensure that it is not overzealous in this regard. Nursing homes have a wide range of policies governing the use of physical restraints. Bedrails are used as physical restraints in some states. Direct that the nursing home provide only the specific physical restraints that the patient needs for their protection.
- **Outdoor Areas:** Are there outdoor areas in which the patients and visitors are permitted to walk and talk?
- **Available Services:** Are there personal care services, such as hairstyling, barbers, manicure, pedicure and other grooming services?
- **Ombudsman:** Contact the ombudsman in your state to obtain specific information on the nursing home you are considering. The facility may have a resident-ombudsman as do many of the state, county and veterans nursing homes.
- **Residents Council:** Does the nursing home have a resident council consisting of patients at the facility? Much like student governments, councils can help to identify problems at the inception and offer suggestions to correct them. The existence of one indicates that the facility is interested in modifying itself according to the needs of

its clients.
- **Medicaid and Medicare:** Is the home certified for Medicare and Medicaid? If so, do they meet federal guidelines?
- **Patient Population:** Does the character of the patient population (e.g., psychiatric, hospice, rehabilitation) appear to be compatible with the patient?
- **Patient Accounts:** What arrangements does the home make with regard to patient's personal savings account? Are able-minded patients allowed to manage their own finances?
- **Theft:** What are the security measures taken by the nursing home administration to protect patients from theft of personal possessions and money?

Step 2: Ensuring Quality of Life for the Patient
- **Visitors:** Family, friends and relatives should make every effort to visit a patient as often as possible once care begins. Visitors should be observant: introduce yourselves to the staff and make sure nurses assigned to the case are personally involved.
- **Listen:** Visitors should listen attentively to a patient. Talk and give the patient your undivided attention. Empathy is most important. Often, nursing home patients are frightened about making a complaint because they fear reprisal. I have conducted several patient abuse investigations in which the alleged victim has refused to speak with me, or with the official supervisor at the nursing home. The patient was concerned about being labeled a troublemaker by the staff.
- **Roommates:** Is the patient compatible with his or her roommate? Many times roommates need time to adjust to each other, but sometimes a change is warranted. If so, demand the change.
- **Food:** A patient with special dietary needs should be monitored to ensure that he or she is receiving the appropriate food. Visitors who bring food to a patient should always check with the dietary or nursing staff first. Many patients are on medicines or prescrip-

tions that may be incompatible with certain food or drink intake.

- **Bathing and Personal Hygiene:** Inquire as to the policy of the nursing home with regard to bathing and personal hygiene. A patient or family should be able to request that, for example, a female patient be bathed by a female aide. The staff at a nursing home is supervised by nurses and all personnel should be trained professionals. However, if you have any specific requests regarding personal care, always make your requests both verbally and in writing.

- **Jewelry and Cash:** Safeguard all jewelry, personal belongings and cash. Nursing home patients move throughout the facility at different times of the day and their rooms are usually open for safety and monitoring reasons, making valuables easy to steal by other patients or by the staff. A visitor who wants to give a patient a gift of money should determine the policy of the nursing home with regard to patient accounts. If accounts are secure, deposit monetary gifts directly into the patient's account.

- **Tipping:** There should be no reason that a patient or visitor should have to tip an employee to care for a patient. An employee who provides outstanding service to a patient should be complimented personally and, in exceptional cases, writing a commendation to the administration of the nursing home.

- **Overtime:** If the staff at a nursing home is consistently working overtime, then the facility is understaffed. If this condition exists, state regulatory agencies should be notified.

Step 3: Handling a Patient Abuse Complaint

Any indication of possible patient abuse should be investigated by the administration of the facility and, if compliance is not forthcoming, by a regulatory agency. Most state attorney generals have a special investigative unit that specializes in the investigation of crimes against the elderly. The address and phone number for your attorney general in your state is listed in the appendix of this book. I worked in New York's version of this unit. Complaints can also be filed with the local police department, state ombudsman and/or the state health department.

An investigator who receives a complaint of patient abuse or other type of allegation will request information regarding the details of the alleged offense. The sample complaint form on the next page will assist potential investigators in their investigation of a complaint.

Step 3: Sample Patient Abuse Complaint Form

Name of Complainant: _____

Address: _____

Phone Number:_____

Patient Name: _____

Age:_____

Date of Birth: _____

Facility Name: _____

Address: _____

Phone Number:_____

Status of Patient: _____

Nature of Complaint: _____

Date of Occurrence/Observation:_____

Description of Complaint:_____

_____

_____

Date and Location of Photographs or Videotapes: _____

_____

Name and Description of Alleged Perpetrator:_____

_____

_____

Names/Descriptions of Witnesses:_____

_____

_____

Next of Kin or Authorized Person Notified: _____

_____

_____

Date: _____

Step 4: Life and Death Decisions

The patient or family must be fully aware of the extent to which rights have been signed over to the health care facility. Life and death decisions are never made by doctors unless a specific directive is made by the patient in advance. Nursing homes request patients (and their families) to make numerous difficult decisions regarding life support and other health care directives. It is very important that patients understand that their directives must be in writing in order for a physician, nursing home, or hospital to comply with their decisions. Patients can direct health providers to take a course of action should they become unable to communicate. When patients complete a health care directive, they authorize a doctor (and nursing home) to remove or not remove them from life-support systems if the patient is in a permanent, irreversible coma. These health directives are subject to a byzantine maze of state regulations and my legal expert, Attorney Steven M. Cohen, gives a comprehensive explanation of these documents in the legal issues chapter.

Jumping to Conclusions

Sometimes even a nice patient and a well-qualified health care worker collide, resulting in serious problems. This happened with Rosie and Mabel.

Rosie was sitting in her chair, staring out her window at the County Community Nursing Home. At age eighty-eight, Rosie still had all of her faculties, but a stroke two years earlier had left her partially paralyzed and unable to live by herself. Rosie had thick gray hair, a thin frail body and a strong personality which she had developed during a long and difficult life.

Mabel was known in the nursing home as "the Road Runner," because she had a sparkling personality and was in constant motion, continually attending to the requests of her patients. Her regular patients anxiously awaited the beginning of her shift. The Road Runner provided a rare type of care—she had a sense of humor. Mabel was a single parent with two teenage sons and was going to nursing school at night to improve her job opportunities. In the last four years, Mabel had been designated "employee of the month" six times.

The Road Runner had put four patients to bed when she entered Rosie's room at 7:35 P.M. Rosie was staring out her window at the setting sun, daydreaming about a family picnic that she was on fifty years ago at Bear Mountain. Mabel went over to assist Rosie, waking her out of the dream. Rosie, shocked to see someone she thought was a stranger, swung her arms at Mabel who blocked the attack and ran for help. She found the charge nurse, Jill, who was well known to Rosie.

Jill then explained to Rosie that Mabel had been at the nursing home for many years and that she was assigned to help her. Jill asked Rosie to cooperate and get into her bed. Mabel then assisted Rosie and helped her get ready for bed. Rosie apologized, stating that deep in a daydream, she had simply forgotten who Mabel was. The Road Runner then proceeded to assist Rosie's roommate Irene, who was partially blind and severely confused, in her nighttime routine.

By the time Rosie's son came to see her the following Tuesday, the incident was forgotten. Jim, however, saw a black and blue mark on his mother's arm and asked, "Mom, what happened?" Rosie had completely forgotten about her attack against Mabel the previous Friday, but she told Jim that one of the aides must have hit her. Such a statement from Rosie was probably simply a subconscious plea to her son to visit more often and to be more attentive. In the end, however, it prompted a criminal investigation of all the staff of the facility, in particular, the Road Runner.

This could have been prevented by the following action:
- Rosie should have told the nursing home that she does not want to be put to bed strictly at 7:30 P.M. Often, patients at a nursing home are intimidated by the rules and regulations and they forget that they have rights.
- Mabel should have tried to move at a moderate pace when she

assisted unfamiliar patients.

- The nursing home should have hired more employees in order to reduce overtime. Unfortunately, in nursing homes, employees often work second eight-hour shifts, increasing the stress for the worker and the patient.
- Jim should have visited his mother more often and asked her if she had any problems with the way she was treated before bruises appeared. Having found that Rosie did not like to be put to bed at 7:30 P.M., Jim could have conveyed his mother's feelings to the supervising nurse.

Overlooking Things

Gail, an eighty-four-year-old patient at the Washington Geriatric Home, had severe diabetes. Often confused and no longer capable of feeding herself, she appeared to be receiving the best quality care under very difficult circumstances. Gail had been losing weight for almost a year, but lately, her weight had stabilized at eighty-four pounds—there was not much hope for recovery. Her daughters, who visited at least three times a week, wanted to make certain that she received care conducive to giving her the best quality of life possible.

Jose, the oldest of five children, had many part-time jobs while he went to high school. For him, college was never an option. He took a special education program and received his certificate as a certified home health aide just after his eighteenth birthday. When the Washington Geriatric Home hired him, Jose was proud of his new job and of the decent salary he would be making.

One Tuesday morning, the charge nurse directed Jose to give Gail a bath and to then weigh her in the tub room. As Gail was not ambulatory, she had to be strapped in a chair which was connected to the scale. Jose began his assignment, transferring his patient from the room to the shower where Gail was undressed, placed in a bath chair and bathed. She was then transferred to the tub chair to be weighed. The shower room and tub room were in close proximity to the nurses' station and the doors were left open to permit nurses to supervise the bathing procedure.

Gail's daughters were horrified to find their delicate mother crying later that day. She tearfully exclaimed, in a moment of lucidity, that she had tried to tell the nurses that under no circumstances was a man to bathe her. The daughters' reactions changed from horror to outrage upon hearing this.

Do you consider this an acceptable procedure? Should an eighteen-year-old young man be bathing an eighty-four-year-old sickly, frail woman despite her wishes? Is it legal? Yes. Can it be prevented? Yes.

You can prevent Gail's problems. Do not overlook any detail of care:
- You have the right to demand that bathing is to be done with two qualified staff members present at all times.
- If you or your patient is concerned about being bathed by a member of the opposite sex, put your request in writing, possibly in the admission agreement.
- Remember when you visit a patient at a nursing home, ask questions, lots of questions. A nursing home patient who suffers from dementia relies on his or her family and friends to act on his or her behalf.

Racism in the Nursing Home

Jack, a contract mechanic, had been a troubleshooter for automotive fleets: if a leasing company or taxi fleet was having a chronic car problem, Jack was the man entrusted with finding a solution. He was a big, loud man with a hearty laugh and a somewhat distorted sense of humor. Most of his working life, Jack used racial, ethnic and religious slurs to describe anyone who was not white or Protestant like himself. He used some discretion in his working years so as to avoid confrontation. Now, Jack, eighty-nine years old, had stopped using racial slurs; however, sometimes he slipped.

Hubert, born in Jamaica, moved to the United States fifteen years ago at the age of twenty-one. This large, well-spoken man had been a certified nursing health aide at the Community Nursing Home for ten years and was well qualified. Since he was assigned only to the male patients, he was sometimes referred to as an orderly. He also worked part-time on weekends as a private duty home aide. Hubert's wife, Elizabeth, also from Jamaica, worked full-time as a nurse at the County Hospital. They had three teenage children who all had reasonable expectations of going to college.

One Thursday, Jack woke up at about 5:00 A.M.—he'd wet his bed, again. As Jack lay in his soaked bed, he felt humiliated by his incontinence. Thinking back on the days when he was the problem solver instead of the problem, he remembered one particular diesel engine that he had rebuilt in three days. Jack was startled to hear Hubert and his partner Charles. As they approached him, Jack became furious when he overheard Hubert tell Charles, "He's wet again!" Jack then lunged at Hubert, throwing punches and yelling racial slurs. Hubert vigorously defended himself and shoved Jack in the chest, causing Jack to lose his breath.

The Community Nursing Home's racial incident could have been prevented:

- If you are elderly now, my simple advice is to stop using insults to describe different ethnic, racial and religious groups immediately. Fortunate enough to have lived a full life, you should realize the utter stupidity of these kinds of insults. Facing dependent care, you need to be aware that the very people that you were unkind to in the past may be your caregivers in the present or future.
- In-service training personnel at the nursing home should constantly remind their staff not to startle patients and to move slowly when first approaching patients.
- In-service trainers should remind staff that many patients are upset about being incontinent. Patients should be assured that this problem occurs to many others.
- Nursing home staff should be reminded that they may be insulted

and abused by their patients on occasion. Staff members must walk away and ask their supervisor to handle the problem. Physical violence toward patients is never justified, no matter what is said—racial, sexual, etc.—it is criminal.

-   Sensitivity training, now widely common in law enforcement and other professions, is a good idea in a nursing home situation. Demand that a home conduct such training, replete with lectures by professionals in the field of sensitivity education, if you are worried that your loved one may be discriminated against.

Chapter 8

The Hospice

Big Jack was a gentle giant who always had time for a friend. Jane did not recognize Jack when she flew across the country to visit him for the first time in the cancer ward at a community hospital in Boston. The frail, thin man that she saw sleeping in the bed by the window could not be her father—she thought that she must be in the wrong room. The man lying in Jack's bed had no hair and looked so old. Her dad was only seventy. *That poor man is much older,* she thought, *it can't be him.*

"Jane, I wanted to die in my own home," whispered her tired father.

Jane struggled to look at the patient in the bed by the window. *He does look a little like Dad, the eyes, mouth and nose are his. Oh my God,* she said to herself, *how did this happen so fast?* Her hero was dying. She was ready to scream. Beginning to cry, Jane told herself, *I must be a good daughter. Please Lord, help me to be calm.* She walked closer to her father. She held his hand. Tears flowed from her eyes. She whispered to the man she finally recognized, "I will take you home, Daddy."

Jack's lung cancer had metastasized and had spread throughout his body. The oncologist, a recognized cancer specialist, had tried everything possible to save her patient, but there were no more options. Big

Jack had, at most, two months to live, more likely two weeks. All Jack wanted to do was go home and spend the last days of his life where he felt he belonged.

The community hospital was affiliated with a not-for-profit hospice which was certified by Medicare and licensed by the state. The hospice medical director, supervising nurse and social work director all conferred with Jack and his daughter about the hospice program. Jack and Jane were familiar with hospice, since Jack's wife Mary had died three years earlier at her home. She had been a patient at the Community Hospice Program. The necessary consent forms were completed at the hospital. Jane made arrangements to have a hospital bed delivered to her father's home Monday morning at 10:00 A.M.

Jane poured her energy into preparing her dad's home for the hospice program. She decided that the hospital bed should be placed in the living room so that Jack could look at the activity in the flower garden in the backyard and also be surrounded by his family. Monday morning was more hectic than Jane had expected. Her brother and sister were both flying home and they were bringing their families with them.

At 9:30 in the morning, Jane decided to go food shopping so that she would not have to leave Jack when the ambulance brought him home. As she left Jack's house, she wrote a note on the front door for the delivery men. She told them that the garage door was open and she wanted the hospital bed to be placed in the living room.

The hospital bed was delivered by two new employees of the rental company. John, the supervisor, drove the truck and carefully backed into the driveway. Jim walked up to the front door and read Jane's note. The delivery men then carried the bed and other portable equipment into the house.

Jim looked around the house. He saw opportunities for theft. No one was home: no witnesses. John started to leave. Jim told him that he was going to use the bathroom. John questioned Jim as to why he was putting on his work gloves (so he wouldn't leave fingerprints).

John ordered Jim to leave the house immediately. Jim left reluctantly, John followed; he locked the door behind him.

In the early afternoon, Jack arrived home by ambulet. He was carried to the hospital bed in his living room. He gave a faint smile to his children, grandchildren and friends. The hospice team stayed with him until he was comfortable in his surroundings. Jack survived three weeks in his home, before he died peacefully in his sleep.

The six steps to prepare for home care, which are defined in Chapter 5, will benefit patients and families who participate in home hospice programs. Those six steps for home care are summarized as follows:

Step 1: Prepare the Home
A safe and comfortable environment should be created for the patient, family, visitors and home care workers. Remove hazards that can cause injuries, such as small step-stools, loose rugs, mats and electrical cords that can cause a fall. Install night lights that will provide a clear path to the bathroom at night. BE THOROUGH!

Step 2: Safeguard Your Possessions
Remove temptation. All cash, jewelry and other valuables should be safeguarded in a protected location, such as a safe deposit box or safe. All financial records, such as bank statements, credit cards and checkbooks, should also be protected. Social security, pension and investment checks should be directly deposited into accounts to prevent loss, theft and forgery.

Step 3: Obtain and Install Medical Equipment
Obtain all of the medical equipment that will assist a hospice patient to be comfortable. The hospice provider should have the experience to assist you with this step. Always bear in mind that obtaining the equipment is the first part, then the equipment must be installed in the home and used by the patient.

Step 4: Selecting the Hospice Worker

A hospice patient or his or her family may need to hire home care workers to assist with the treatment of patient care. The hospice program may be able to assist you in the selection process. You should always check with your insurance carrier to determine the limitations of your coverage. If you decide to hire a home care worker independently, be careful! Review Chapter 5 and follow the screening process before you allow a stranger to enter your home. Prepare for a telephone interview first and obtain specific information such as professional license numbers, experience and references. Do not agree to pay "off-the-books." Arrange to meet all acceptable candidates in a neutral location, after you have verified the information that they provided in the telephone interview.

Step 5: Employment Application

Require the hospice worker to complete a detailed employment application. See the sample application in Chapter 5.

Step 6: Respite Care

The hospice caregivers and patients benefit from respite care. Many hospice and palliative care programs provide respite care for the patient and caregivers. It is very important that patients and caregivers communicate with the hospice team, especially if they are fatigued emotionally or physically. Review and use the respite services listed in Chapter 5, along with the respite services provided by your hospice program.

Hospice Care

Medicare, the primary insurer of senior citizens, added a hospice benefit in November of 1983. The Medicare hospice benefit provides limited funding for qualified terminally ill patients. Two doctors must agree that a patient's life expectancy is six months or less in order to apply for the benefit. The other qualifying criteria will be explained later in this chapter. The Medicare benefit has had a major impact on the acceptance and growth of hospice and palliative care programs. In 1980, there were approximately 200 hospice programs in the United States. By 1996, that number had increased to more than 2,400 hospice and palliative care programs.

Any elder patient with a terminal illness can choose to enter a hospice program. Approximately 70 percent of all hospice patients are over the age of sixty-five, while many are diagnosed with cancer, hospice services are available to patients with other illnesses. The hospice philosophy accepts the approaching death of a patient and does not offer a cure or recovery, but rather hospice attempts to provide a comfortable and pain-free environment for the patient. Hospice attempts to assist both the patient and the family to make the most of the limited time that they have together. A hospice coordinates many disciplines of health care, including doctors, nurses, social workers, health aides, chaplains and volunteers.

There are many dedicated health professionals who provide compassion and assistance to hospice patients. The emotional trauma of impending death is felt by family, friends, health care workers and most importantly, by the patient. This is a time that a patient and his or her family are vulnerable to fraud. Fortunately, most hospice programs have rigorous recruiting procedures and they have not experienced many fraud complaints. However, as our population ages, there will be more demands placed on the resources of hospice programs. Therefore, patients and families will have to be more vigilant to protect themselves.

The emotional and physical demands of hospice care require a program which selects only exceptional caregivers. They have to screen their applicants to select the employees who can provide compassion and withstand the stress of providing care to dying patients. Palliative care is the soothing of the symptoms of a disease without effecting a cure. Hospice care is often referred to as palliative care.

Hospice programs treat the patient and family by providing trained professionals who give bereavement assistance during the emotional trauma of comforting a dying patient. In addition, a hospice provides bereavement services to friends and family after the death of a patient. The emotional benefit of hospice care is that the patient accepts that he or she is near death and does not want aggressive curative medical intervention to prolong his or her life.

Hospice care can be provided to a dying patient in the following ways:
- **Hospice at Home:** Most hospice care is provided to dying patients in the home. The hospice program will assess the home and trained professionals are placed with the family to provide a comfortable environment.
- **Hospice Residence:** Provides hospice care to dying patients who do not require inpatient hospital care but are unable to live in their own homes.
- **Hospice in Nursing Home:** Some hospice programs have made arrangements with nursing homes to provide hospice care at a nursing home for dying patients who are not able to remain in their own homes.
- **Hospice in Hospital:** Inpatient hospice care is provided at the hospital for patients who cannot be treated at home.
- **Hospice Day Care Program:** A hospice patient continues to live at home, but is transported to the hospice program during business hours to receive emotional comfort and social support.

Each hospice attempts to empower dying patients and to give them control of how they want to spend their remaining days. Although Medicare and certain private insurance policies cover hospice services, their coverage is limited. Home hospice programs usually provide intermittent services that are designed to supplement and assist the dying patient and their family.

The home hospice does not usually provide full-time day and night coverage. Instead, the hospice team makes periodic visits to assess and review the condition of both the patient and family. A nurse, social worker or other trained hospice worker will address the needs of the family, answer questions and make practical suggestions based on their experience and training.

The hospice team is available twenty-four hours a day to respond to emergencies, but much of the day-to-day care is provided by friends or family. There are many situations when a patient hires a home health aide or nurse at his or her own expense to assist with the maintenance care. There are many long-term insurance policies that cover this service.

The first priority for many hospice patients is the relief of pain. The hospice team has the education and experience to assist the patients with the proper drugs and physical therapy to help them to find comfort and at the same time remain alert. In addition, the hospice program may provide the portable medical equipment that will permit the patient to remain comfortable in his or her own home.

Medicare Coverage of Hospice Care

Medicare will only pay for services provided by a certified hospice, which provides the following hospice services (usually on an intermittent basis):
- Doctors' services
- Nursing services
- Drugs, including outpatient drugs for pain relief and symptom management
- Physical Therapy, Occupational Therapy and Speech Language Pathology
- Home health aid and homemaker services
- Medical social services
- Medical supplies and services
- Short-term inpatient care, including respite care
- Counseling

**Services not provided by Medicare when provided
by a hospice:**
- Treatments other than for pain relief and symptom management
  of a terminal illness.

The Medicare hospice program was designed as a six-month program. The government estimate was that many of the patients would live close to six months, with some patients living beyond that time period. Medicare continues to cover patients who live past their life expectancy, as long as the patient's care remains within the criteria of the program. The reimbursement schedule for hospice has taken into account that there should be a balance between the financial gain at the beginning of the hospice treatment and the financial loss during the intensive demand for service just prior to death. However, since the average duration of hospice service for qualified patients has been slightly under two months, many programs have experienced financial difficulties.

To qualify for the hospice benefit in Medicare and many private insurance programs, a patient must meet certain admission requirements, such as the following:
- **Medicare or Insurance Eligibility:** The patient must be insured.
- **Doctor(s) Diagnosis:** At least one doctor, usually two, must diagnose that the patient has a terminal illness and the prognosis is that the patient has six months or less to live.
- **Comfort Oriented Care:** The patient must want to receive comfort oriented care and not curative care. The patient and their family must consent in writing that they desire hospice care.
- **Doctor's Consent:** The patient's doctor must agree that the patient should receive hospice care.
- **Hospice Setting:** must be safe for the patient.
- **Do Not Resuscitate (DNR):** A DNR order is required by some hospice programs. A DNR is explained in detail by Attorney Steven M. Cohen in the legal issues chapter. Basically, a DNR means that

no heroic intervention such as CPR will be provided by the hospice program.

- **Limitations:** Some hospice programs limit their coverage to their specific membership, such as Health Maintenance Organizations, Veterans Administration or a limited geographic boundary which is accessible to their staff.

Remember: a good hospice program provides respite care for both the patient and the family. Fatigue, both physical and emotional, can increase the stress for the patient and caregiver. Respite services can provide the relief that is needed to accept the many challenges of the dying process. Families and patients should share their problems with the hospice team in order to reduce stress.

The Long Ride Home

On December 23rd, two days before Christmas, Jane discovered that she could no longer get out of her bed. Three years of secret chemotherapy and other cancer treatments would now become known to her adult children. Maybe they would be able to smile someday in the future, when they would learn that their mother's monthly "union meting" was a disguise for her doctor appointments. Unfortunately, on this day, Jane had to share her terminal illness with her family.

Jane was a protective single parent who had been a widow for almost thirty-five years. She kept her illness to herself as her last gift to her family; fortunately, they had known of her cancer and were able to provide her with subtle support, while at the same time protecting her secret.

When Jane called her sons and daughters to take her to the hospital, the family was ready. The six adult children and their spouses had already developed a plan to care for "Mama." They had expected that she would have surgery and return to her home.

It was too late for a surgeon—this seventy-six-year-old patient was beyond any conventional cure. Jane's doctor told her and her family that she was terminally ill and that she could expect to live six days to six weeks; he recommended a hospice-at-home program.

The hospital bed was placed in Jane's bedroom which was on the first floor of the house. The first week at home the house was filled with a constant flow of friends and family. Jane loved the activity and with the help of the pain medication, could sleep through any of the usual social activities of her visitors. The hospice team included a doctor, nurse and social worker to educate the family about Jane's care. A daughter and granddaughter moved in with Jane to provide full-time care. The hospice provided a daily home health aide for a four-hour shift.

During the first two weeks, family and friends provided Jane with the full-time care that she needed. Jane was bed-bound, pain-free and a cooperative patient. Also, Jane's condition had stabilized; she was alive and alert. However, her daughter Sally had to go back to work, her granddaughter had to go back to school and the insurance only paid for a four-hour shift.

Amy, the oldest daughter, was in charge of Jane's finances. Jane had $23,000 in the bank, her house was paid for with no outstanding mortgage and she had an income from her employer for a medical disability. Amy called the hospice program and asked to increase the home health aide shift to eight hours from Monday to Friday. The additional twenty hours per week would have to be paid for privately since it was not covered by Medicare or private insurance. The next two weeks were hectic for Jane's family, as her daughter struggled to get home before the end of the eight-hour shift. Jane's condition remained stable. Amy decided to increase the home health aide shift to ten hours, two five-hour shifts.

Four months later, Jane remained stable, but her bank account was just under ten thousand dollars. Amy reviewed Jane's life insurance policy and found that it contained a *Living-Needs-Benefit*, also known as an *Accelerated Death Benefit*. This is an option which allows a terminally ill policyholder to receive a portion of the life insurance policy (usually between ninety to ninety-five percent of the benefit) prior to their death.

Jane began to worry that her hospice benefit would expire since she had outlived her six-month life expectancy. This issue was addressed when the hospice social worker visited Jane and Amy. Since two of Jane's doctors continued to diagnose that Jane's condition had not improved and that her prognosis was terminal, the Medicare hospice benefit continued beyond the six-month time period.

Eight months later, Jane's condition remained unchanged and her bank account had dwindled to a mere two thousand dollars. Even though Amy was able to reduce the home health aide shift to eight hours, the expense of the home care was still higher than the income. Amy and her brother decided to use their own money to cover any additional costs. They expected to be reimbursed in full from the proceeds of their mother's life insurance and, if necessary, from the expected sale of Jane's house.

Jane died peacefully in her own home a year and a half after she entered the hospice program.

When a hospice patient lives beyond six months:

- Prepare both a short-term and a long-term plan. Discuss all possibilities with the members of the hospice team, in particular, your social worker. These professionals often have the experience to guide you through an unexpected crisis.
- Contact your insurance company periodically, to determine the status of your coverage for hospice services.
- Remember, even if you have Medicare or insurance coverage, the patient is often financially responsible for part of the health services.
- Contact the patient's attorney, accountant and insurance agent *before* you initiate any major financial transactions.
- Use the hospice support services that are available for patients, caregivers and families.

The following organizations can provide additional information regarding hospice care:

Hospice Education Institute
190 Westbrook Road
Essex, CT 06426-1511
(800) 767-1620

National Hospice Organization
1901 N. Moore Street
Suite 901
Arlington, VA 22209
(800) 658-8898

Hospice Association of America
(A subsidiary of the National Association for Home Care)
519 C Street NE
Washington, D.C. 20002
(202) 546-4759

Academy of Hospice Physicians
500 9th Street N.
Suite 200
Saint Petersburg, FL 33075
(813) 823-8899

National Consumers League
815 15th Street NW
Suite 928-N
Washington, D.C. 20005
(202) 639-8140

American Cancer Society
1599 Clifton Road
Atlanta, GA 30329
(800) 227-2345

Widowed Person's Service
American Association of Retired Persons
601 E Street NW
Washington, D.C. 20049
(202) 434-2260

 **Chapter 9**

Legal Issues:
An Interview with
Attorney Steven M. Cohen

The hospital emergency room is not the place or time to make difficult life and death decisions. Unfortunately for many patients, they have not prepared for an emergency and therefore, either they or their family must make critical decisions in a time of stress. Today, we live in a complex world, in which people can control their own destiny if they have prepared a life plan. The more I learned about elder care, the more questions I had for Attorney Steven M. Cohen, an established elder law specialist.

My first comprehensive interview with Steven lasted almost twelve hours. I had prepared an extensive list of elder care questions based on my research and life experience. Steve answered my questions in two ways: first he would give a clear and precise explanation of the legal issue, then he would tell a story about a real-life application of the subject and the importance of understanding the law. As you have probably gathered, his style is very much like mine.

The chapter that follows, I feel certain, demonstrates on its own the professionalism and competence of Steven Cohen. He has intentionally given life to some issues that we sometimes believe only happen to the other guy. Elder abuse and fraud happens to all of us.

Steven M. Cohen has achieved numerous professional accomplishments. He is a full partner of the firm of Lorenzo & Cohen, a member of the Erie County Bar Association, the Association of Trial Lawyers of America, the New York State Bar Association, the New York State Trial Lawyers Association and the American Bar Association. He is admitted to practice before the Supreme Court of the State of New York, the United States Tax Court, the United States Bankruptcy Court and the United States District Court.

Q. When should a client seek the advice of an attorney about an estate plan?
A. To answer this, we ought to examine what exactly it is that an attorney can do for a client in an estate context. Anyone who has a need for the services outlined below should certainly consult with a lawyer. A lawyer can assist a client with, among other things:

First, the drafting of a binding last will and testament which effectively gives a client's property away specifically to the people and charities the client chooses following his or her death. Every state has laws which determine exactly how a person's property is disposed of if he or she dies with no valid will. People to whom a client would like to leave a certain item, sum of money or property may not get it unless the client has a will which specifically provides for that bequest. A last will and testament can also leave instructions to guide family members regarding burial agreements and the type of funeral service the deceased would have wanted.

Let's look at a few cases in which a person failed to execute a properly drawn or current last will and testament and his or her wishes were not carried out after his or her death.

A sixty-two-year-old woman had an engagement ring which she very much wanted to give to a favorite niece upon her death. She had always intended to give the ring to that niece and it had been promised to the niece over the years. She also had an antique brooch which had passed from mother to daughter for four generations. She wanted to pass the brooch to her daughter and her daughter was promised it over the years, consistent with the family tradition. The woman unexpectedly passed away without having executed a will. The laws of her particular state provided that the engagement ring, the brooch and everything else in the woman's estate had to go to her hus-band—to whom she was unhappily married—and who happened to dislike that particular niece and wasn't on speaking terms with the daughter. The ring ended up on the finger of the husband's mistress and the brooch on the mistress' lapel. The spirit of the woman is undoubtedly restless to this day and there was no recourse for the niece or daughter. A simple will directing that the ring pass to the niece and the brooch pass to the daughter would have seen to it that the wishes of the deceased were carried out.

In another case, a young husband, Harry and his wife, Helen, had a son whom they named James. They purchased a "Last Will and Testament Kit" from a stationery store to save the money a lawyer would have charged. They followed the instructions carefully. If either spouse died, his or her assets were to go to the surviving spouse. If the spouse had already passed away, the assets would go to the son James. They properly signed the "reciprocal wills" in the presence of the required number of witnesses. After the will was made, Harry and Helen had their second son Paul.

When Harry reached seventy, he took ill with emphysema, severe arthritis and diabetes and the wife cared for her husband at their home.

Growing up, Harry's son James was always in some sort of trou-ble and in heavy debt. James borrowed large sums of money from Harry and Helen over the years, which he never repaid. James rarely came around, even in later years, and then only when he needed money. He never came to visit socially. Paul was financially secure, married and had a stable middle-class lifestyle and never borrowed money from Harry and Helen. Paul and James were on poor terms with one another.

As Harry's illnesses became worse, Paul helped Helen care for him. For years, Paul would come over almost daily and help Harry bathe and dress. Paul would look after the maintenance of the house and help with the heavy chores. Helen was stricken with a spinal disc degenerative problem when she was seventy-eight and was rendered unable to care for Harry or herself without daily assistance. Paul had Harry and Helen move in with his family, all of whom helped to care for the aging couple.

Harry passed away and there was no probate proceeding. Helen passed away and all assets went to James. Paul and his family received nothing.

Second, a lawyer can assist with tax planning to minimize the state and federal governments' interest in an estate, which maximizes the property available to go to the people and entities of the client's choosing. Sometimes adverse tax consequences can be avoided by very simple standard language in a will, language which goes unnoticed and unappreciated unless it is *absent* from a will.

For example, it is common to put a provision in a will which states that if a beneficiary dies within ninety days of a decedent, he or she will be considered to have predeceased or died before, the testator. Let me show you a situation I came across in which that common provision was not put in a couple's otherwise well-drafted wills and there were devastating tax consequences.

Guy and Gail worked hard to raise their two children and to see to it that the family would be financially secure. Guy worked outside the home earning a salary and also receiving company stock as regular bonuses, while Gail raised the kids at home, managed the money and established a diversified portfolio worth about $350,000. Guy had a $750,000 life insurance policy naming his estate as the beneficiary. Gail had received money from a personal injury lawsuit when the couple was in their early fifties which fully paid off their home, which had a value of about $200,000. Guy and Gail's other property, collections, artwork, etc. had a combined value of about $50,000. Guy and Gail were driving with their twenty-four-year-old son and their recently married twenty-six-year-old daughter one winter evening. They were on their way home from a golden wedding anniversary party for a great-aunt for which the children came into town to attend with their parents. They were driving in the son's new car. The daughter's husband and two-week-old baby were at home. There was a one-car accident leaving Guy dead and Gail and the son and daughter severely injured and hospitalized. Gail died several hours after she arrived at the hospital. The son died two days later and the daughter died three weeks later.

Guy's will provided for everything to go to Gail. If Gail predeceased Guy, the entire estate was to pass to his surviving children equally. Gail's will provided for essentially the same thing. Neither will contained a provision for a person to be considered to have predeceased the testator if he or she died within ninety days of the testator.

The entire estate, worth about $1,350,000 (including the life insurance policy) passed to Gail without taxable consequence, but a probate proceeding was necessary to pass title of the entire estate to Gail. The estate then passed from Gail to both children. Federal estate taxes were approximately $300,000 and state death taxes were approximately $125,000. After taxes, attorneys and court costs, the son and daughter each received about $400,000. Out of the son's bequest came college loan repayment of about $20,000 and car loan payment of about $12,000.

Since Guy's son died without a will, the laws of his state provided for everything to pass to his sister. A public administrator was appointed, taxes were paid in the amount of about $38,000, lawyers and court costs were paid and about $325,000 went to the daughter (his sister) from his bequest. Her student loans were paid off and other unsecured debts satisfied. The daughter also had no will so the approximately $710,000 she received, after being taxed on state and federal levels, caused her husband and baby to end up with approximately $550,000. Had Guy's will contained the appropriate provision, the daughter's husband and baby would have ended up with approximately

$900,000 after all funeral expenses, taxes, attorneys and court costs. Also, the time it took for the estates to completely resolve would have been much shorter and far less of a headache for the young husband of the daughter, upon whose head everything fell to resolve. *You see, had the provision been put in the will that anyone dying within ninety days of the testator would be considered to have predeceased the testator, the estate would have gone directly from Guy to the baby.*

Third, a lawyer can set up creative trusts which regulate the way in which property passes to different entities, minors, etc. in accordance with the client's specific instructions. Rather than passing money directly to a person or charity in a lump sum to be spent at the free discretion of the beneficiary, you can provide for a more regulated gift. For instance, it is common to provide that a child under twenty-one years of age be given money to be used for educational purposes only, with the remainder given to him or her after he or she reaches the age of twenty-five years. You can also provide that the educational "trust fund" may be used by the intended beneficiary for medical emergencies, room and board, etc. In this way, a testator can prevent the temptation to convert a bequest into a car in favor of education. There are many kinds of trusts, each with its own unique tax consequences and each allows the testator to have some control over assets, even after death, by leaving carefully crafted instructions as to how the money is to be spent.

Fourth, a lawyer helps in the preparation of documents which authorize a trusted friend or relative to make medical decisions for clients in the event of their incapacity and which give instructions to hospitals as to the type of heroic measures clients may or may not want if they are in a permanent vegetative state or afflicted with a terminal illness with no chance of cure. Health care proxies, living wills and "do-not-resuscitate" orders differ from last wills and testaments in that they take effect during the life of a person, whereas a will only takes effect after death. A lawyer can draft all of these documents for a client.

Fifth, assistance is provided in the transfer of a client's assets prior to death to avoid probate. The inter-vivos or "living" trusts can effectively dispose of all assets so that all of a person's property is given away during his or her lifetime, with the client retaining the right to use the property until death. When the client (grantor) dies, there is nothing to probate and nothing for the state and federal governments to tax. Deeds of gift and planned exempt gifts can accomplish the same goals, without the grantor retaining use for his or her lifetime.

Sixth, a lawyer is necessary in the financial planning in anticipation of long-term care in a nursing facility. The laws of every state differ with regard to this. An attorney can advise clients about how best to protect assets prior to going into a nursing home. This may include timed conveyances of property, long-term health care insurance, private pay arrangements, certain public assistance, etc.

Seventh, aid is available when a person is applying for the various benefits available for health care, nursing care, utility costs, food and shelter.

Eighth, a lawyer prepares documents which authorize a trusted and competent person to act on behalf of the client in financial and legal matters (power of attorney).

Finally, a lawyer is crucial during various court proceedings: for the administration of an estate, probate of a will, defending/contesting the validity of a will or applying for/defending against the appointment of a committee or guardian to assume control over the assets and affairs of an alleged incompetent person.

Q. What is a living will?
A. We touched upon this a little bit earlier. A living will is simply a carefully thought out set of written instructions to health care providers as to precisely what treatment patients want or don't want if they are ever unable to make those decisions at a later time. In every state, competent adult patients have the absolute right to make decisions regarding

their medical treatment. While patients cannot order their own death in the event of suffering, they can certainly refuse to take certain medications which would serve only to prolong agony and they can request medication which might ease their pain. The problem is that at the time that these very decisions need to be made, patients are often not thinking clearly or are otherwise unable to communicate their feelings to their health care providers. A living will is a formally executed document which is prepared when a client can think clearly, giving directions to doctors and hospitals in such situations. Living wills are binding in many jurisdictions and not binding in others. Different jurisdictions have different requirements regarding the formality of the execution of the living will, such as the presence of witnesses, notary public, physician, etc.

There are a few things which a client needs to remember. First of all, a living will only has an effect when the client is alive, just as a last will and testament only has effect after death. After death, the living will has no legal meaning. Therefore, you wouldn't ever want to combine the two documents into a single document. Secondly, a clear thinking patient can certainly overrule or "revoke" the living will by speaking up at any time. It is not intended to bind patients to any course of medical action, but to serve as the voice of patients when their voice is otherwise silenced by infirmity or mental competence. Lucid people may make the decision that they would never want to be on a respirator for the rest of their lives, being kept artificially alive at great expense, while in an irreversible coma. Once in the coma, patients can hardly let their feelings be known. Therefore, the living will does the talking for them.

Q. What is a DNR order?

A. "DNR" stands for "do not resuscitate." Along the lines we just mentioned, if clients lives are reduced to constant suffering, they may not want their life prolonged if they ever lapsed into cardiac arrest. This might be relevant for people with advanced terminal illnesses who don't want their family's money spent on artificial life support like respirators when their death is inevitable and they will never again regain consciousness. Individuals might want to be "allowed" to pass away peacefully and without technology, keeping them technically alive but in a vegetative state. They can leave instructions to loved ones in a living will that they want no heroic measures taken to prolong a painful life and ask that if they are ever in cardiac arrest, that no one performs CPR or other lifesaving techniques. The problem is, paramedics and other emergency personnel and health care providers who come to the aid of a person in cardiac arrest have a legal duty to try to save that person. This is where a DNR order comes in. A DNR order is a legal document which, in the states which allow them, instructs health care providers not to perform CPR or other heroic resuscitative efforts. A DNR order specifically absolves health care providers from responsibility for withholding resuscitative measures. Generally, a DNR order must be co-signed by both a licensed physician and either the person to whom the DNR order will apply or his or her "health care proxy," who is a person designated to make life and medical decisions for that person.

Some states have detailed legislation authorizing DNR orders and specifically protecting health care providers who honor those orders. A DNR order is not to be mistaken for any sort of request by a patient to be *put* to death by a care provider. To the contrary, a DNR order provides that if patients should lapse into cardiac arrest or "death," they are to be left alone. It is generally up to the co-signing physician to carefully review the medical prognosis with the patient before signing the DNR order. The physician should make absolutely certain that the patient knows the meaning and magnitude of signing a DNR order.

Q.   When do you need to prepare a will?
A.   In my opinion, a will should be executed any time clients want their assets to be handled differently upon their death than the laws of their jurisdiction provide for in the absence of a will or if they have specific instructions they want followed after their death. In other words, young parents may want a will to provide for a guardian for their

children in the case both parents pass away. They may want to establish education trusts for the kids rather than allowing the estate to pass unrestricted to the kids as soon as they are of age. In essence, a will give a people one last time to speak and direct their own affairs, even after death.

People may think they need a will and it is quite possible that their attorney may have an alternate solution to the person's estate problem. In fact, a document called a living trust is sometimes a better alternative than a will, since it spares the beneficiaries and loved ones the task of probating a will. I always recommend to people that when they see their attorneys, they should simply state their goals and allow the lawyer to advise the best way to go about reaching the stated goals.

If I may broaden the scope of your question a bit, rather than advising just when a party needs a will, here's a list detailing when people need to see their attorneys.

When to see an attorney:
 1. After bearing or adopting children;
 2. When they believe they may, at some point in the future, need nursing home care;
 3. If they have specific requests concerning their medical treatment or if they should become unable to make decisions for themselves or communicate on their own behalf;
 4. If they have specific people or organizations they want to leave property to after their death who would not be a beneficiary without a valid last will and testament;
 5. If they want to appoint someone to have the authority to make important medical decisions for them if they are unable to make such decisions for themselves or otherwise communicate their wishes;
 6. If they have specific burial or funeral instructions to be followed;
 7. If they believe their assets will exceed the federal and state tax thresholds, such that there will be tax consequences upon their death;

8. If they need to explore different benefit options offered by their county, state or federal government which they do not understand and which haven't been adequately explained to them by public officials;

9. If they wish to avoid the complicated probate process by giving away assets before their death through the use of tools, such as living trusts and inter-vivos gifts;

10. Anytime an immediate family member passes away with an estate which needs to be administered (no will) or probated (a will exists);

11. Anytime they have legal concerns about their estate.

As I said before, certain estate goals are often better addressed with tools other than a will so it is important to tell your attorney precisely what you want to accomplish and let the lawyer give you the available options.

Q. When does a beneficiary learn the contents of a will?

A. After the death of the testator. When people die, their will is hopefully brought to the attention of a lawyer or the court. The lawyer will then put everyone mentioned in the will on notice of the passing of the person and of the existence of the will. It is common practice to send a copy of the will to the relatives who would be entitled to the decedent's assets if there was no will (i.e., spouse and children in most jurisdictions) plus all people named in the will as a beneficiary, executor, guardian or trustee, but that is not required by the laws of all states. In some areas, beneficiaries and immediate family may simply be summoned or "cited" to appear at a will reading or to court to examine the will and be given the opportunity to object to the will. Sometimes, a testator will put something in the will called an "*in terrorem*" clause which provides that a beneficiary will lose their bequest if he or she objects to the will. The practice of formal will readings where the family gathers together with named beneficiaries to hear the contents of a will for the first time has more or less given way to the more common procedure of mailing certified copies to all named parties. When there are several wills by the same person, beneficiaries are given the opportunity to object to the will that is offered for probate in favor of an earlier will, if they can show good cause. Earlier wills are often sent to the beneficiaries as well for their examination and are certainly available for inspection by parties and their attorneys.

Since the existence of multiple wills which have been made by a person from time to time tend to cause conflict, it is generally a good idea to destroy all old wills once a new one has been executed.

Q.   Do beneficiaries know if a will has been changed?
A.   If a will has a *codicil* or amendment, both the will and the codicil will be sent to the beneficiaries after the death of the testator. If there are old wills in existence, they too will be sent to all the beneficiaries if they are found. In some jurisdictions, beneficiaries may only be advised of the existence of older wills, but may not be provided with copies for their examination and they may need to appear in court when the latest will is offered for probate in order to gain access to the older wills.

Q.   Do family members and beneficiaries get notified when someone changes the will?
A.   No. A will is a very personal thing and there can be no undue pressure, coercion or influence over the testator when they are drafting a will. To notify family members of changes being made to a will would be to stir up hornet nests which would cause the very pressures the law forbids. No one except the testator and the lawyer need to know the contents of a will until the testator passes away.

Q.   What happens if a client becomes too confused to care for him or herself?
A.   The court can appoint a person or group of people to look after the affairs of people who have become too confused to manage their own matters or otherwise take care of themselves. These appointed care-takers are sometimes called *conservators, committees* or *guardians.* They will

often see to the hiring of nurses and other caretakers for the person or may have the person admitted to a long-term health care facility. If clients are concerned about their own abilities to continue to manage their affairs in the future, they can appoint and authorize a trusted individual to take on that responsibility before they actually lose the ability to think clearly. By appointing an *attorney in fact* through the use of a special document called a power of attorney (as opposed to a licensed attorney at law) to handle one's affairs, they can avoid the need for the court to intervene with the appointment of a committee or conservator.

Q. What is a power of attorney?
A.   This is the document by which people authorize another to act on their behalves. Powers of attorney can be general, authorizing the "attorney in fact" to act in all matters in the place and stead of the "principal," or it can be highly specific. For example, people can sign a power of attorney authorizing a friend to list a house for sale and then convey the house for them. Let's say John will be moving out of town and he wants his home sold. He can execute a power of attorney empowering his friend Samantha to act on his behalf regarding the sale of the home. Samantha can then contact a realtor, sign a listing agreement, review any offers, accept an offer and then actually sign the deed conveying the home to a purchaser, noting on the deed that she is signing as an "attorney in fact" or as "power of attorney" for John. The actual power of attorney form would have to be recorded at a nominal fee along with the deed to ensure clear title to the purchaser.

Let's take it a step further. John is concerned about his abilities to continue to manage his affairs on a day-to-day basis. He is tired and has periods of confusion. When he is thinking clearly, he contacts his attorney and asks for a power of attorney appointing Samantha as his general power of attorney. The form can specify that Samantha is authorized to act on John's behalf of all matters and it can further specify that if John should ever become incompetent, Samantha shall continue to have authority to act for him. The form is signed by John and notarized. Now, Samantha may manage John's legal, financial and day-to-day affairs acting with the full authority of John. Remember that a power of attorney is only valid as long as the principal is alive. *It does not take the place of a will and* if John were to pass away, Samantha would be powerless to dispose of John's assets or manage his affairs. Until John's death, if the power of attorney has been so drafted, Samantha could be empowered to act for John in all matters and transactions. Of course, John could revoke the power of attorney at any time. If the power of attorney is on record with a county clerk or city recorder, John should record the revocation with the same office to make a public record of the revocation.

Q. What financial abilities does a power of attorney grant?

A.   The most important reasons to have a power of attorney—if you have someone you completely trust with all of the powers a power of attorney conveys—are to give your agent or *attorney in fact* the ability to engage in Medicaid planning, in asset management associated with Medicaid entitlement and in the various spousal impoverishment acts which most states have to protect the spouse of someone who needs costly long-term health care. This means giving your *attorney in fact* full power to manage, transfer, convey, sell, purchase, gift and otherwise dispose of your assets. That takes a lot of trust and not everyone is fortunate enough to have people in their lives upon whom they can comfortably give all of that authority. A dishonest or unqualified agent or *attorney in fact* can do a great deal of damage to a principle's estate so be sure of the person you select. Otherwise, the court can appoint guardians, committees and conservators to oversee and manage your affairs and the court will scrutinize the actions taken by such people to insure an honest accounting. If you are lucky enough to have a qualified, trustworthy friend or relative who is willing to take on the responsibilities as your *attorney in fact*, you should strongly consider speaking with your attorney about executing a power of attorney.

Some states have standard power of attorney forms which list the types of transactions and affairs the *attorney in fact* can handle for the principal and which require the principal to actually initial before the authority to handle such a matter is given to that person. Some forms give the full range of powers to the *attorney in fact* unless otherwise limited to only certain transactions by a specific notation by the principal. The nature of and complications associated with the power of attorney form really require the attention of an attorney at law before a principal executes such a powerful document. It would be a shame for John to have gone to the lengths of obtaining, executing and filing a power of attorney during his competency only to have it declared invalid during his later incompetency because a simple box wasn't checked off or if the form did not pass muster with the latest state statutory requirements.

Q.   What makes up an estate plan?
A.   In my opinion, almost everyone should have an estate plan which includes:

1.   A power of attorney which authorizes another to fully act in the event of incompetency.
2.   A health care proxy which authorizes someone to specifically make health care decisions in the event of incapacity.
3.   A living will which sets forth the desires of the principal regarding life support, organ donation, heroic rescue measures, etc.
4.   A last will and testament. As stated earlier, having a validly drawn and executed power of attorney can avoid the need for the appointment of a guardian, committee or conservator, a process which is not only costly, but also emotionally draining on loved ones.

As an additional safeguard, you may wish to appoint joint agents as your *attorneys in fact*, a provision which requires two or more people to act together and unanimously when making decisions for you. For financial powers of attorney which are executed specifically for the purpose of allowing others to make business type decisions for you, appointing joint *attorneys in fact* can be very useful. First of all, you get the benefit of the judgment and experience of two people for every decision made on your behalf. Secondly, each can monitor the other to prevent a dishonest transaction.

The laws of every state are different and an attorney should be consulted to make sure the form you are using complies with the formality required by your state.

Q. What is a "durable" power of attorney?

A. The term "durable" power of attorney refers to a power of attorney which allows the *attorney in fact* to continue to act for the principal after the principal becomes incompetent. It is said to "survive" the incompetence of the principal. Whereas an ordinary power of attorney form may have a provision for it to survive the principal's incompetence if a special box is checked or initialed, a document labeled "Durable Power of Attorney" will generally affirmatively state that it will survive the principal's incompetence or incapacity unless the principal specifically checks off a box or specifically initials a provision which renders the power of attorney void in the event of incompetence. A "non-durable" power of attorney or one which does not specifically provide for the principal's incompetence, is a power of attorney intended only as a matter of convenience for the principal during their absence or periods of occupation with other affairs, but which is based upon the notion of ultimate control resting with the principal. In the example of John and Samantha, I discussed earlier, John would have ultimate control of his affairs and could monitor Samantha's actions at all times, ultimately revoking her authority if and when that became appropriate.

For estate purposes, a "durable" power of attorney which survives the incompetence of the principal is far more useful than one which becomes void upon incompetence. Medicaid planning, estate management, etc. after incompetence can save you and your spouse a great deal of grief and money. Along the same lines, a "springing" power of attorney is a power of attorney which specifically and only takes effect upon the incompetence of the principal. It is generally held in escrow by a lawyer until the client becomes incompetent or incapacitated, upon which the lawyer contacts the *attorney in fact* and presents the duly executed springing power of attorney form.

Q. What is a durable power of attorney for health care?
A. The health care power of attorney is a power of attorney which gives someone full authority to make medical treatment decisions for you when you are unable to make such decisions for yourself. Many states have provisions for health care proxies which do the same thing as health care powers of attorney.

Q. Is a power of attorney recognized only in the state where it was drawn?
A. This differs from state to state. As a general rule, other states will honor a power of attorney if it has been drafted and executed in such a way that it would have been valid if it were drafted and executed in that other particular state. Let's say state one requires that the power of attorney be notarized and state two requires two witnesses plus a notary of the principal's signature. A power of attorney executed in state two would most likely be accepted in state one, but the reverse is not necessarily true. If you advise your attorney that you expect to eventually reside in another state, the formality required by that other state can be quickly researched and the power of attorney can be executed in such a way as to pass muster with the requirements of both the state you are in and the state you intend to reside in eventually.

Q. What advice would you give to a family in an elder care crisis?
A. If at all possible, steps should be taken prior to a crisis to plan for the likely scenarios associated with the elderly. An elder care crisis can put a whole family into a state of emotional confusion. It is at this time that an attorney can come to the rescue by organizing and dealing with whatever problems come along. The advantage of bringing in an attorney at such a time lies in the fact that the lawyer is emotionally detached from the situation and can act with a clear head. Of course, it would be more

prudent to have a plan laid out prior to the crisis in anticipation of the crisis or death or disability of a loved one. If an attorney isn't available at the time of the crisis, a trusted friend or clergyman should be called who could help bring the chaos under control. Sometimes it just takes a calm person on the scene of a crisis to ask the important questions and write down the answers on a pad to effectively bring a crisis situation into clear focus.

Family lawyers with whom you have a relationship will often make themselves available on weekends and late night hours in times of need. You should keep the telephone numbers of lawyers, clergy and close friends handy, not just for your own use, but for use by people who may come into your home when you are incapacitated and may want to reach out to your support network on your behalf.

If you are in the midst of a crisis involving an elderly friend or relative, I would suggest the following:

1. Get help. Call your attorney, friend, clergyman, police department, fire department, relative, neighbor, etc. If you are frazzled, having someone around to assist or even just to hold can be invaluable.2.
2. Locate necessary documents, such as medical insurance cards, wills, health care proxies, DNR orders, powers of attorney, medical records, etc.
3. If you must leave the house to accompany someone to the hospital, turn off anything on the stove, coffee pots, etc., bring change for a pay phone and money for a meal (and a taxi ride home if you travel to the hospital by ambulance or emergency vehicle). Take your personal telephone directory and don't be afraid to call collect. Go to the bathroom before you leave and take any of your own medications you may need with you. Bring your glasses.

Q. What do you do if someone has passed away in your home?
A. First of all, it is important to stay calm. A thousand questions race through your mind when faced with this situation. You should call the rescue squad or paramedics as soon as you find an unresponsive person. He or she may not actually be deceased and the rescue personnel can render

immediate treatment if warranted. If the person is deceased, the rescue personnel can and often will transport the deceased to a hospital, which can easily and efficiently deal with the administrative details of the physical body. If a rescue squad isn't available, call the police. If you've called the fire department or rescue squad, chances are a police unit has been simultaneously dispatched. The police have ready access to anyone else who may be needed, like the medical examiner or funeral director. There are a few things you *should not* do if someone passes away in your home. Although you may want to preserve the dignity of a friend or loved one who has passed away, resist the temptation of moving or dressing a body before the rescue squad or police arrive. There is no shame in death and the location of the person when he or she is found by you may give the police or medical examiner a clue as to the cause of death. Even if he or she is on the toilet or in a state of undress, leave the person undisturbed until the authorities arrive. Of course, if you are administering CPR or other first aid as part of a rescue attempt, you should certainly move the person to the extent necessary to properly care for him or her. After you have called rescue squad or the police, you may want to notify the clergy representing the faith of the person. Clergy are often a calming influence, whether they are administering some religious last rites or comforting loved ones.

Q. Can a person be too sick to draft a will?

A. If a person is of sound mind, he or she can execute a valid last will and testament. Even if he or she is paralyzed and cannot sign their name, a person of sound mind with the aid of qualified witnesses can execute a valid will. People who are not of sound mind and who are not thinking clearly *cannot* execute a valid last will and testament, even if they are physically fit and have witnesses. People must be able to convince witnesses that they know that the document they are signing is their will, they must know what the will is for, to whom they are making bequests, who they are appointing as executors and trustees, what the responsibilities are of the executors and trustees, the nature and extent of their bounty and their own identity. They must be able to convince the witnesses that no one is coercing them or exerting a force or influence which is in any way interfering with the testator's free choice.

I can recall a situation a few years ago when a family contacted me after their elderly brother passed away. A will was produced which, to everyone's amazement, left everything to a lady who lived next door to the brother. Although they knew of the woman and knew she was a friend to the decedent, it struck everyone as odd that his whole estate would go to her to the exclusion of the family, which had been close knit and supportive of one another for eighty years. At the will contest trial, I put the attorney who drafted and witnessed the will on the stand, followed by his secretary, who also witnessed the will. The following information came out in testimony:

1. The lady went to the attorney and told him her friend was in the hospital and wanted to draft a will.

2. The lady handed the attorney a sheet of paper with all of the provisions her friend supposedly wanted in the will, which of course, left everything to her and appointed her executrix. The paper was in her handwriting and was supposedly dictated by the decedent to her.

3. The lawyer drafted the will in accordance with the terms on the paper, went to the hospital with his secretary and read the will to the man approximately one week before his death and had him sign the will.

4. At the time of the execution of the will, the decedent had an IV (intravenous) in place administering morphine sulfate.

5. At the time of the execution of the will, the decedent spoke very little English. He was of Italian descent and Italian was his first language.

6. His signature was not recognizable and literally dropped off the page.

7. The woman was present in the hospital room at the will reading and execution.

8. The woman paid the attorney fees.

9. Neither the attorney nor his secretary could recall the decedent saying anything at all. They didn't know if he had an accent and

didn't know the sound of his voice. They based their attestation of the decedent's competence on a slight nod of the head.

Needless to say, the will was thrown out. Even if the decedent had spoken English, the will could be challenged because he was on medication which could be said to have dulled his faculties at the time of the execution of the will. Even if he spoke English and wasn't currently on medication, the will could be challenged because of his illness which caused him great pain and rendered him exhausted and distracted. In short, a will is too important a document to leave to the last minute and your situation may eventually deteriorate such that you cannot execute a valid will when you finally get around to it.

Q.   What if you can't afford an attorney?
A.   Almost every jurisdiction in the United States has an organized bar association which has a program that provides free legal services to people who qualify. In addition, just about every attorney I know does a certain amount of *pro-bono* work for people who cannot afford to pay. Start with the bar association in your area. If you can't find one, call your state bar association for guidance.

Q.   Do you have any other advice that you feel would make things easier for a family that has experienced the loss of a loved one?
A.   One thing that I try to impress upon everyone is to keep all important papers in one place and to tell your executor and lawyer where those papers are kept. I'm specifically talking about your will, bank books, bank records, life insurance policies, health care proxy, powers of attorney, living will, securities portfolio records, records of monies owed to you by others and information on the whereabouts of all assets and a listing of all account numbers. Tracing that information down can be very burdensome.

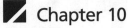 **Chapter 10**

Financial Issues:
An Interview with Kathy Adams,
Certified Public Accountant

Financial issues are significant at every stage in our lives and they reach a pinnacle during our senior years. Retirement, social security, pensions, long-term care, bills, estate planning—such are the stuff of many a nightmare.

Elder care is a challenging situation for patients and families. The complicated regulations of various government agencies at the federal, state and local levels add to the confusion.

Kathy Adams is a certified public accountant (CPA) and a management consultant. She has the experience and knowledge to help a patient or family with the difficult financial issues associated with elder care.

Some people are left destitute after paying for dependent care, while others in similar circumstances are not. In many ways we are a very private society, especially when it comes to our finances. Elder care can be extremely expensive; long-term care can impoverish an individual or family. Kathy Adams, a leader in her field, who is always on the cutting edge of financial and accounting issues. I am grateful that she has taken the time to share her financial wisdom in the following pages of this book.

Kathy Adams describes how financial professionals, like herself, are often frustrated when clients do not fully understand the consequences of their actions. As you read the financial advice provided by Kathy Adams, I am certain you will understand the importance of consulting a financial expert and understanding your options, *before* you make what is often a difficult decision to change.

Kathy Adams is a partner with her sister, Diane Jaskot, in the accounting firm of Adams & Jaskot. Kathy has received numerous honors and awards, including the 1992 March of Dimes Women of Distinction Award. She is a member of the National Association of Women Business Owners, the New York State Society of CPAs, the American Institute of Certified Public Accountants and the National Conference of CPA Practitioners.

Q. When should a client address elder care issues with an accountant?
A. Planning ahead is always a good idea, well before there appears to be a need. A good time to begin the dialogue might be when you are having your income tax return prepared by your accountant. Ask your accountant about his or her experience in the area of elder care and estate planning. If your accountant does that as part of his or her practice, set up an appointment for a consultation, preferably after April 15, when your accountant will be more available. If your tax preparer does not have experience in this area, seek a referral to someone who does.

Q. What are the advantages of estate and financial planning?
A. Planning in advance of a crisis can help to avoid potentially costly mistakes. Once the plan is created, it takes time to implement because there are restrictions on how much you can give away and when you can give it. For instance, any gifts or transfers of property within the three years prior to the date of the death can still be considered part of the estate for estate tax purposes, even though those assets were no longer in the possession of the decedent.

When someone has worked their whole life and accumulated assets, it is a tragedy to see those assets disbursed to pay medical expenses and estate taxes. The higher a person's net worth, the more complicated the planning can be, but someone whose only asset is their home should make sure that asset is protected. Careful planning can ensure that more of these assets are available for the surviving spouse, as well as the children and grandchildren.

Q. How can an accountant assist a family during an elder care crisis?
A. Protecting assets often means shifting ownership between family members. Any change of ownership other than between husband and wife can have significant tax implications. Making decisions without proper advice can be costly.

A father who was dying of cancer knew that he was within days of his death and wanted to make things easier on his son. Both the father and the son figured that it would be easier to transfer assets while the father was still alive. So they went to a lawyer and had the father's house transferred to the son. A week later, the father died. The house, which was worth about $150,000, was included in the father's estate, because the transfer was made within three years of the date of death. No federal estate taxes were due, only state. If the son had inherited the house, his basis in the house would have been $150,000 and when the house was sold, no capital gains tax would be due. However, since the house was a "gift," his basis in the house, according to the tax code, was the same as the father's, $40,000, which was what his father had paid for the house. When the house was sold for $150,000, the son had a taxable gain of $110,000. This mistake cost the son more than $35,000.

A one-hour consultation with an accountant or an estate tax attorney would have cost between $150-$250 and would have avoided this whole problem.

Q. Can estate planning help reduce inheritance taxes?

A.   Yes. One spouse can leave all of his or her assets to the other with no tax. In addition, each person is entitled to an exemption and can (currently) leave up to a million dollars or more without paying any estate tax.If an estate is worth several million dollars, it is important for a married couple to understand that they can develop a plan that will allow each of them to use their exemption. For example, if the husband dies, leaving everything to his wife, no tax is due. Then, when the wife dies, her taxable estate will be reduced by only her exemption. However, if the husband had distributed assets (within his exemption amount) in his will to his children, either directly or through a trust and left the remaining estate to his wife, then no taxes would be due at the time of the husband's death. Then when the wife dies, her taxable estate would be reduced by her exemption.

Federal estate taxes can be as high as 55%. If the estate consists primarily of real estate or a family business, often there is not enough cash to pay the taxes without liquidating assets. This problem can be solved by making sure there is enough life insurance to pay the tax. If someone has accumulated a lot of assets, there may be a need to set up one or more trusts. This is a legal maneuver done with both your accountant and lawyer working together. Each situation brings a different set of facts and circumstances and may require a different solution.

Q. Do all states impose the same inheritance taxes?

A.   Estate tax regulations vary greatly from state to state. Don't make any assumptions about what the rules are, especially if you retire in a different state or your parents live in a different state. Make sure you know something about the laws in the state where you or your parents are residing. After someone dies, you may find out something you didn't want to know about the local estate tax regulations.

Q. What happens when a person maintains two separate geographic residences?

A. If a person dies with homes in two states, they may end up paying estate taxes in both states, even though one state truly was their principal residence. New York State, for example, firmly believes that once a New Yorker, always a New Yorker. If a person retires from New York and moves to Florida but keeps his or her home in New York, he or she may be a New York non-resident for income tax purposes and if he or she dies owning real estate in New York, New York will consider them a New York resident. New York actually went so far as to say that if you owned a burial plot in New York, you were a New York resident! After all, it shows that you intended to return to New York permanently, therefore, New York was truly your home.

Q. What are the limits on tax exempt gifts?
A. People are very often confused by the gift tax laws. If, in 2004, someone gives a gift of more than $11,000, the person giving the gift is required to pay gift tax. The person receiving the gift does not pay tax on the gift.

A person may give a gift of up to $11,000 in any calendar year without incurring any tax. Therefore, a husband and wife can give up to $22,000 to each of their children without incurring any tax. A person can give unlimited gifts of up to $11,000 per person during a calendar year.

This is why tax planning is important. It may take years to give away assets to the children so that no tax is incurred.

Q. Can a child claim an elder parent as a dependent?
A. If the parent's gross income does not exceed the IRS limit, (excluding tax-exempt income and social security) *and* the child pays for more than one-half of the parent's support, the child may claim the parent as a dependent, even if the parent does not live with the child.

Q. Can an elder parent's medical expenses be claimed as a tax deduction?

A. If the parent is a dependent and the taxpayer has paid the parent's medical expenses, those expenses can be taken as a tax deduction.

Q. Is life insurance subject to inheritance tax?

A. Life insurance may be subject to estate tax. It depends on who owns the policy. When the person who dies owns a policy on his own life, leaving someone else, i.e., a child as beneficiary, the money goes to the child tax-free. However, the amount of the policy is still included in the estate. Now if the child was also the owner of the policy, even if the parent paid the premiums, the entire policy would fall outside of the estate and no tax would be due. Life insurance that is part of an employee benefit plan may be taxable to both the beneficiary and the estate.

Q. Are pension plans, IRA's, 401K's, etc., subject to inheritance tax?

A. Yes. In addition, they may be taxable to the beneficiary.

Q. What are the tax implications for a surviving spouse?

A. Generally, transfers between spouses have no tax sequences so almost everything will pass to the spouse tax-free. Life insurance proceeds from an employee benefit plan are taxable on the amount in excess of $5,000. Proceeds from a spouse's IRA may be rolled over to an IRA by the surviving spouse.

Q. Are burial costs and probate fees subject to inheritance tax?

A. Funeral expenses, probate fees, attorney's fees and accounting fees are all deductible for estate tax purposes.

Q. What advice would you give to a family in an elder care crisis?

A. Don't try to make decisions without appropriate advice. Because there are so many rules in this area, you will need an attorney and an accountant and possibly an insurance professional to *work together* to make sure nothing is overlooked. Put together a team of professionals who are compassionate, understanding and knowledgeable about your situation. Make sure everyone is clear about the goals and objectives. What makes sense from a financial or legal point of view may start a family feud that no one anticipated.

Creating a plan before the crisis will make a difficult time just that much less stressful. If you are already in a crisis situation, you may have missed some very important opportunities, but that doesn't mean there is nothing you can do. Make sure that you have explored all of your options.

Q.   How often should an estate plan be reviewed?
A.   With the almost constant changes in tax laws, it is necessary to make sure you keep your estate plan current. Changes put into the tax code in 2001, for example, will phase in over a period of years. Then when everyone has planned according to what is current, the law will sunset in 2010 and will revert back to the rules that existed prior to the changes made in 2001. It is impossible to predict how many changes may occur between now and that point. Sound confusing?

Seek professional advice. Ask your accountant every year if there have been any changes in the estate tax law about which you should be concerned. There is no timetable that says to review your current plan every, say, three years. It is simply a matter of keeping current with tax law changes and changes in your personal circumstances.

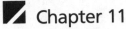 Chapter 11

Health Issues:
An Interview with
Dr. Lynn M Tepper, Gerontologist

Columbia-Presbyterian Hospital is located in New York City on the west side of Manhattan and is one of the busiest and finest hospitals in the country. The faculty and staff at Columbia-Presbyterian Hospital have earned a global reputation for excellence in the health care community.

I waited patiently in the crowded lobby of this hospital for the opportunity to meet a recognized leader in gerontology, Dr. Lynn M. Tepper. I was not surprised that Dr. Tepper was pressed for time when we started our scheduled meeting; her patients and students, as expected, came first. However, she was very enthusiastic about the opportunity to participate.

Gerontology is the comprehensive study of old age and the aging process. The physical, social and economic needs of the elderly are studied by a gerontologist. Our population is growing older in record numbers. The senior citizens of today are the pioneer's for the "baby-boom" generation. Dr. Tepper is an energetic leader in identifying and solving the problems of the elderly.

I discussed the difficulty and challenges that confront our elder population with Dr. Tepper. She answered every question that I asked with knowledge and authority. In addition, she told me of many additional elder issues that she had experienced in her practice and in her research.

I thought about the magnitude of the transition that is taking shape in our society as we step into the twenty-first century. There are problems and there are solutions. My life experience has taught me to respect experts in their field of study. I am grateful to Dr. Tepper for sharing her experience with us.

I encourage any patient or family to seek the health care professionals who are experts in gerontology during any elder care crisis. Actually, I urge you to seek out a person, such as Dr. Tepper, before an elder care crisis. These professionals have the experience and knowledge to guide a patient to the best plan of care.

Dr. Tepper is Associate Clinical Professor of Columbia University, School of Public Health and Director of the Institute of Gerontology at Mercy College. She holds a Doctorate in Gerontology from Columbia University and is a Fellow of the Gerontological Society of America. Dr. Tepper was a delegate to a White House Conference on Aging, serving on the Committee for Health Care Policy.

In the following pages, Dr. Lynn Tepper will provide insights into some of the difficult challenges confronting the elder population.

Q. Why did you study gerontology?

A. I studied gerontology for many reasons. As a doctoral student in the 1970s in the Department of Counseling Psychology, I realized that the growing number of older people in this country would require expertise in this area, especially as it relates to mental health concerns of this population. Although part of me saw the handwriting on the wall, another important consideration was my sincere admiration and respect for the wisdom that existed among our elders, as well as the keen insight they have into solving life's problems.

Q. Do senior citizens have special needs?

A. Yes and no. A majority of older people will experience little, if any, change in their activities of daily living. Most have reached old age because they are "survivors," surviving diseases and conditions for which there were no treatments or cures, considering they reached middle age before medical technology was as advanced as it is today. Even so, most can spend their later years in relatively good health, perhaps declining rapidly at the very end of life. Only a minority—perhaps 20%—will spend their last years with needs that require full-time intervention by caregivers. And only a fraction of those will require institutional long-term care. Most of their needs are very much like anyone's needs, that is, to be informed about what is happening next. In order to increase quality of life, senior citizens need to be informed about things like enticements, benefits and programs. The needs in old age also are those relating to legal and health issues, which may change somewhat. Knowing about a living will, a health care proxy and advance directives such as DNRs (do not resuscitate) and such issues that will effect how they choose to die, will help the aging process run smoothly.

Q. Have you observed that different generations (cohort groups) respond in a unique way to aging?
A. Yes, indeed. This present generation is referred to as the "New Old" in some of the gerontological literature. They are new in that they are the best educated, have the highest income and are in the best of health of *any* past generation of older persons. The next generation of older persons—the "baby boomers"—will be even more so. They will be the largest group to ever reach old age and we know that in numbers, there is strength! They are doing all kinds of things to fight old age or shall I say the potential ravages of old age! They exercise, eat cautiously, watch their sodium, fats, etc. They also are very much in the mainstream of life. They are politically active (AARP has more control of health care legislation than we may think!).

Q. Do environmental factors such as alcohol, substance abuse, prescription drugs, smoking and obesity effect the elder population?
A. These environmental factors effect them as they do younger people, but in old age, we begin to see the results of years of damage. A lifetime of alcohol abuse often leads to Korsakoff's Dementia even

before old age, in fact. We are also seeing alcohol abuse happen for the first time in old age, as a response to loneliness, losses and isolation and a future that is not promising in some cases. We now know that our lifestyle decisions in young and middle age results in some of the chronic, long-term illnesses and debilitation we see in old age. Smoking, obesity, a diet high in fat and sodium content and inactivity often lead to cancer, heart disease, emphysema and neurological disorders. Prescription drugs can effect mood, behavior and mental status if used incorrectly and the elderly take an average of 6.5 different medications each day!

Q. When should a person start to plan for a dependent living arrangement?

A. Very few of us will ever plan for a dependent living arrangement. Among the elderly I see, dependency is one of their greatest fears. It just happens and plans are seldom in place. Perhaps sometime in one's sixties or seventies, discovering an environment that is less demanding should be considered. The recent growth in CCRC's (Continuing Care Retirement Communities) shows that this is happening. You "buy-in" able to play eighteen holes of golf and plan to "age-in-place," thereby remaining there until the very end. These places usually have home health care and long-term care on their premises.

Q. Who can assist a patient or family during an elder care crisis?

A. I find that a variety of professionals are helpful, usually working together in collaboration, to assist in a crisis situation. If it is health related, usually the physician is involved at first. Then rehabilitation services, such as physical therapists and occupational therapists, are helpful in assisting the elder to reach a higher level of functioning. Social workers are terrific at obtaining concrete services and accessing benefits and entitlement. Many provide support to the family as well as the elder. Psychologists and psychiatrists are helpful in assessing mental status and making sure that what seems to be dementia really *is* dementia and not something totally or partially treatable or even reversible.

Q.   What are some of the problems you have found with home care?

A.   The biggest problems I've found with home care occur when the elder or spouse or the family (whoever accesses this service) does not find a licensed, registered home health care agency to supply the care in the home. Getting someone out of the newspaper can be a disaster—even *with* referrals! Making sure these caregivers are trained to provide care is important. Also, home health care needs to be organized and coordinated. There may be a need for three or four different kinds of services to be brought into the home. A new profession is that of "Geriatric Care Manager," a person who knows the ins-and-outs of coordinate care.

Q.   Many senior citizens today have considerable assets. How does this effect elder issues?

A.   I have seen elders become victims in scams and taken advantage of by people they thought they trusted. They and their families should be informed about the existence of these people. Having assets also effects other things. Elders with assets can get better health care in some cases. The poor often are on Medicaid and have to rely on public hospitals and clinics for care. It certainly helps to have a few dollars in old age. If you need long-term care, you may have a choice about where you go.

Q.   Do you have any suggestions for a friend or family member who wants to discuss sensitive issues with an elder, such as nursing homes and finances?

A.   Yes. Be open and honest about these things. For sure, most elders have thought about these things. Some have desires *not* to be institutionalized and some (believe it or not) would not mind or even request placement, rather than be a burden to their relatives or friends. It is important to discuss these things in advance of health crises. Finances are also important to discuss, especially among this generation of elders that consider finances an extremely private matter. Even if it's just telling a family member where important papers are, such as the bank accounts, wills, legal papers and where the safe-deposit box is, would be important to know in case of a crisis.

Q. What is long-term insurance?
A.   long-term care insurance is a relatively new concept. It is insurance for use in long-term care situations, when care will probably be necessary for a very long time or forever. It can protect the family assets by paying for home health care and institutional care, which can be quite expensive (some nursing homes in the New York area are over $90,000 per year). Sometimes care in the home can be cheaper and sometimes more pleasant than a nursing home as the family can be there, with familiar surroundings and more privacy. We should probably purchase a long-term care policy in our forties or fifties, as the longer we wait, the more expensive it becomes. Just make sure there is a cost-of-living benefit which accounts for the rising cost of care each year.

Q. Are there more women than men in nursing homes?
A.   Yes, indeed there are more women than men! In fact, the ratio is now 5:1 in the average home for the aged. This is for many reasons. First, women have a longer life expectancy than men. Also, men often remarry after being widowed so there is often another woman to take care of them. Some new research indicates also that men (fathers) are more likely to be taken care of in the home of their daughters or sons than women (mothers). By the way, it is usually the daughter that provides care, rather than the son. It's a continuation of the nurturing role expected of women...even twenty years after the women's movement!

Q. What is a hospice?

A. A hospice is an environment for those near death, usually within six months or so of death. It is usually in a non-medical environment, without hospital beds and hospital furniture and has arrangements for the family to visit anytime or even stay overnight. Some hospices can be in the person's home so family can be there all the time and various services are brought in.

Q. How important are family and friends when a patient is homebound or in a nursing home?

A. Family and friends are very important to those that are homebound or in institutions. They are the only link the elder has with the outside world and he or she is usually very interested in what everyone is doing.

Q. Do caregivers need support?

A. Caregivers absolutely need support! They also need respite as part of this support, in order to be better caregivers. My book, *Respite Care Programs, Problems and Solutions* (Charles Press, Philadelphia) provides some of the important information relevant to caregiving needs. There are specific support groups and programs that can be accessed for this purpose. Stress management is also necessary for caregivers.

Q. What would you recommend to a patient or family in an elder care crisis?

A. I would recommend that they think clearly—or find someone who does—about what specific things need to be done. They need to view the situation as one that can definitely improve with the right interventions at the right time. The field of gerontology has brought attention to the fact that help is there if you know where to go. Again, social workers, physicians, clergy and the local Office on Aging in their community has some answers to these complex questions.

Q.   Finally, Dr. Tepper you have done extensive research into the difference between memory loss and dementia. What did you learn?

A.   There are many who are fearful that growing old means losing the ability to think, remember or reason appropriately. They worry that when they feel confused or forgetful that this is the first sign of what used to be called "senility." They remember that many years ago, doctors dismissed memory loss and confusion as a normal part of aging. However, scientists have now found that most older people live into late old age alert and capable. They know that people who do experience major changes in their personality, behavior or skills may be suffering from a brain disease called dementia.

The term dementia is used to describe a group of symptoms that are usually caused by changes in the normal activity of very delicate brain cells. Dementia seriously interferes with a person's ability to carry out his or her daily activities. It is irreversible, unable to be cured, but treatable to make life easier for the patient and the family. However, there are many conditions with symptoms that look like dementia, but are not. These reversible conditions can be caused by problems such as high fever, improper nutrition, dehydration, a bad reaction to medicine, a fall or a minor head injury. Although not dementia, medical problems like these can be serious and should be treated by a doctor as soon as possible.

Sometimes older people have emotional problems that are mistaken for dementia. Feeling sad, lonely, anxious or even bored may be more common for older people facing adjustments related to retirement or handling the death of a relative or friend. Adapting to changes at any age can leave people feeling confused or forgetful. Emotional problems can be helped by supportive friends and family, by professional help, by a counselor or with medication.

People who think that they might have a form of dementia should have a thorough physical, neurological and psychological evaluation. This includes a complete medical examination with lab oratory tests, as well as tests of the person's mental abilities. Some tests, such as CAT Scan of the brain, can help the doctor rule out a disorder that can be cured. Even if the scan is normal, it may be useful for comparative purposes in years to come. A complete medical examination also includes getting information about the person's medical history, including their use of prescription and over-the-counter medicines, their dietary intake and recent events in their life that may be related to their emotional state. Because a correct diagnosis depends on recalling these details accurately, the doctor may also ask a close relative for information.

Developing interests, hobbies and staying involved in activities which keep the mind and body active, are among the best ways that older people can remain sharp and keep their mental abilities. Careful attention to physical fitness, including a balanced diet, may also go a long way to help people maintain a healthy state of mind. Some physical and mental changes occur with age, even in healthy persons, but much anxiety and suffering can be avoided if older persons and their families realize that dementia is a disease, not part of normal aging.

Chapter 12

Diversity in Elder Care

The traditional, family-centered support for aging parents and older relatives is no longer possible for many Americans. A combination of factors, such as an increasing number of older people, longer life expectancies and a dramatic increase in the number of dual income families has made it unfeasible to rely on the support of a family. Institutional care, especially in a nursing home, is the choice of last resort for most Americans. However, for first or second generation Americans from various backgrounds, such as the Hispanic or Asian culture, elder care presents additional challenges. By way of example, in this chapter, one of Dr. Lynn M. Tepper's colleagues at Columbia University, Zoila E. Noguerole, has been kind enough to share her story.

Zoila E. Noguerole: A Daughter's Story

In January 2000, I scheduled a follow-up appointment for my mother, who was then eighty-nine, with her neurologist. Although my mother had wandered in New York City on three previous occasions, her latest episode was the most serious. She had attended Sunday Mass in our community and then gone "home" to an apartment she had not lived in for more than twenty years. On that Sunday, after six hours of wandering, she had been spotted and assisted by a group of Jehovah's

Witnesses who had noticed that she looked frightened, tired and confused. Upon approaching her, my mother had informed them that she lived in the neighborhood but could not find her building. These kind strangers took my mother into their place of worship, but found she could not remember her name or mine. My mother was wearing an I.D. bracelet with the 800 number for the Alzheimer's Association, but they had been reluctant to search her. Instead, they were able to help her remember that she carried a small telephone book and then they started to read one name at a time to her until she recognized my name.

Late that Sunday afternoon, I picked up the telephone to hear a stranger ask if I knew Clemencia Núñez. I told them I was her daughter and asked where she was. When they stated their address, I knew immediately that my mother had been searching for her previous home, since the address was one block from where my mother had raised us many years previously. How she traveled fifteen miles on foot from her new home is still a mystery. When my husband and I arrived, I saw how frightened, sad and confused she was as she repeated, "I kept walking, walking and walking and I couldn't find my building." All I could do was hug her, reassure her, thank the people who had helped her and then take her home. And I realized that what the neurologist had recommended eighteen months earlier—that my mother needed twenty-four hour care due to her increasing dementia—could not be postponed any longer. Each time she had wandered in the past, she had been helped by strangers, but I knew that she might not be so lucky next time. Upon arriving at her apartment, located one block from ours, I helped her change her clothes and eat. I told her gently that I could not do any more, that she required more care and supervision than what we could provide, since my husband and I were both employed. I understood I could not protect her from her advancing dementia and so I made an appointment with her neurologist. I remember that during the appointment my mother kept wringing her hands, but sat impassively when I broke down and cried as I acknowledged that this decision could not be postponed any longer.

Because of her diagnosis several years earlier, I had attended meetings for caregivers given by the Alzheimer's Association and followed their recommendation to obtain a durable power of attorney. I also read some of their material to learn more about the symptoms of dementia and which documents I eventually would need to apply to Medicaid to obtain in my mother's behalf. That year, when she was hospitalized for pneumonia and prior to her discharge, I requested the assistance of a social worker who arranged for help through the Visiting Nurse Service. The nurse assigned to her follow-up care checked her health and also authorized an aide for a few weeks. At the same time I filed an application for Medicaid in her behalf and for extended assistance by an aide. Due to the information and reading I had done earlier, I already had the documents necessary for her Medicaid application; both the Medicaid and an aide were approved within six weeks. Over the next eighteen months, my mother had a series of aides, each with varying degrees of skill. The last one assigned to her was extremely kind and competent, though she had the challenge of caring for my mother while she became increasingly ill and belligerent. In an effort to prove she could still be independent, my mother defied the aide by running away from her—on one occasion running into traffic and narrowly avoiding being hit by a car.

My mother, who had raised two daughters alone, worked as a cookie packer until her retirement and enjoyed dancing, the theater, movies, shopping, all of which she reached by public transportation in New York City. Slowly, everything changed. She misplaced or hid gifts and money and, when she could not remember where she had hidden the items, would call me to accuse friends or members of the family of stealing from her. At first I believed her, but when I began to find the "missing" items around her home, I realized that she was hiding them and forgetting their locations. When she accused me of stealing, I became angry and hurt: angry because she did not realize how hard I was working to protect her and hurt because I felt she did not appreciate my efforts.

Faced with the dangers of her wandering episodes, I sought the guidance of a geriatric specialist. On her recommendation, I visited three nursing homes, each of which had distinct advantages and disadvantages. During each visit, my husband and I viewed rooms, dining and recreation areas and chapels and received literature about each facility. I asked where residents would be hospitalized when they became ill. Each visit ended in a meeting with an administrator, with whom we discussed my mother's illness and during which, invariably, I would cry, thinking of my mother's loss of independence. In my family, this decision represented the first break from our Latino culture's tradition, wherein older people always lived with their daughters or sons. However, at that point I had slowly acknowledged that my mother needed twenty-four hour care, that her needs would increase over time and that both my husband and I had to keep working. In addition, my only sister lived out of state and, therefore, was unavailable to help.

How did we select the nursing home for my mother? After the visits, I read the information given to us, reviewed my notes, checked with government agencies to determine if there were complaints against any of the nursing homes and spoke with sons and daughters whose parents were in each of the three facilities. I also spoke with two good friends who also had to make decisions about nursing home care for their parents. Then I shared the information with my mother and sister. Throughout it all, my mother kept insisting that it was "not time yet." Due to its distance from our home, I had eliminated one facility and my sister agreed to come to New York and visit the two "finalists." Thus, in the spring of 2000, my mother and her aide, my sister, my husband and I visited two nursing facilities. At the end of the day we asked my mother for her preference. My sister and I reviewed our rankings, and realized we had all selected the same facility. The skilled nursing facility we chose was spotless, the rooms were comfortable, it was barely five minutes from my home and I, therefore, knew I could continue to visit my mother frequently and check on her care. As an added benefit, the nursing home agreed that if my mother required hospitalization, she could be transferred to the medical center where she had received her medical care for the past fifty years. And, finally, this facility had a beautiful Catholic chapel. Since she had always been a devout Catholic, we hoped that our mother would find consolation and support in the facility.

Barely six weeks after our visits and selection of a nursing home and while still in her own apartment, my mother developed pneumonia and required hospitalization, during which she was evaluated by both her physician and a social worker. Both recommended transfer from the hospital to the nursing care facility. A bed was available and the nursing care facility agreed to accept my mother as a resident. I had already alerted my sister about our mother's hospitalization and she arrived in New York with her husband to help with our mother's transfer. Together, we faced our mother's anger at the fact that her two daughters had arranged to have her admitted to a nursing home. She hurled invectives and expressed her feelings of betrayal and anger at us. She protested that she had never done this to her mother (her mother had lived in Ecuador). We tried to reassure her that she needed this level of care, but she could not understand the toll that dementia was taking on her and on us.

And so we accompanied her to the nursing home and together withstood her ire. We knew how ill she was and that she would not improve. We were frightened for her safety. We were grateful that the social worker and admissions personnel at the nursing facility were kind and reassuring to her and to us. But her sorrow and bitterness left us shaken and sad that we had been forced to take this painful step for her own sake.

A few days later, my sister returned home and I continued in my role of principal caregiver. Although the nursing facility provides good comprehensive care for my mother, my responsibilities certainly have not ended, they simply have changed. I visit my mother, speak with the nurses and doctors and I am still actively involved with her well-being. Some visits are extremely difficult, because I see my mother's continuing decline and because she continues to be angry and bitter. On her most recent visit to our home for Thanksgiving, we noticed that she was beginning to forget her grandsons. She has forgotten much about her daughters' lives and always seems surprised when I tell her about our families or our work. She does not remember the hospitalizations, transfusions or medical care she has received since her admission to the nursing facility and her frailty is increasing more rapidly. We recently had to tell her that her last surviving brother had died, but mercifully she forgot this within five minutes. We take our grandchildren to visit her and she enjoys visits with her great-grandchildren, but she forgets them as soon as they step out of her room. My sister recently reported to me that she feels our mother is beginning to forget her also. It is a consolation to me that despite her anger, she still knows who I am and that she has occasionally thanked me for everything I do. Not all of our visits are pleasant, but the nurses reassure me whenever I speak with them. I have also availed myself of help from a professional to sort out the conflicted feelings I have had over the past few years.

Being my mother's principal caregiver has been rewarding, challenging, humbling and stressful; it has forced me to examine my attitudes and fears about getting older, becoming ill, and dying. It has taken me many months to acknowledge and understand that my mother, once healthy, active and a gadabout, now has multiple illnesses, has difficulty walking and has lost her independence. At ninety-one years of age, she has joined the ranks of the oldest old. I look at her and feel compassion for her and fear that her state presages my own. I remind myself that it is not her fault that she is old and ill.

Since my mother's admission, I've been told by relatives and friends that in our Latino culture we do not place our parents in nursing facilities. That may still be true of families in our homelands, where generations of families live under one roof. It is also true of some families in the United States. But many other families, Latinos included, have had to place parents in nursing facilities. So when I hear this criticism, I ask them if they have visited nursing facilities to see how many Latino residents are present and I also remind them that they have not walked in my shoes. This decision—which was one of the hardest we had to make, which weighed on my conscience, which has caused bitterness and anger—is one that my mother still cannot acknowledge as having been necessary for her safety. My mother is well cared for and she is safe. That safety is consolation and comfort to her family, conflicted though it may be.

We Can All Learn from Zoila

As I read Zoila's elder care experience, I understood why Dr. Tepper suggested that Zoila is the best person to tell her own story. As someone who lives, feels and continues to address many of the complex issues associated with elder care, her experience has special meaning. I have great admiration for Zoila, her mother and her family. In difficult times they have each other and many wonderful memories. To help better understand elder care issues, Dr. Tepper has shared her thoughts on the following questions.

Q.   Why is wandering part of Alzheimer's Disease and related dementing disorders?
A.   Past memory often becomes much clearer than recent memory in the dementia patient. Often they wander in search of an older memory, in Zoila's mother's case, a previous home.

Q.   Why do dementia patients often repeat phrases over and over?
A.   Neurological changes associated with dementia often cause behavioral and physical changes which did not previous exist. This repetitive verbal behavior is an example of fixated ideas that may represent troublesome thoughts and experiences.

Q.   Why isn't the need for 24-hour a day care apparent earlier and often postponed by family caregivers?
A.   Denial is a very normal and common reaction to a loved one's loss of capabilities. The family assumes the individual will remain stable for

longer periods. It is a common phenomena that a crisis situation occurs before this 24-hour a day care plan is activated.

Q. How and why are professional organizations such as Alzheimer's Disease and Related Disorders Association (ADRDA) helpful to the caregiver?

A. Families almost always cannot provide all the necessary attention needed by dementia patients. Many families feel guilty about asking others to help, especially those from cultures in which parent care responsibilities have been expected in previous generations. Seeking outside resources is essential to prevent the burnout associated with the incredible demands of caregiving.

Q. Why do many families go though several paid caregivers before finding one who works?

A. Although this process of finding the right match between a patient and a caregiver is often frustrating, waiting for the right one is essential. The chemistry must be right, because the level of personal interaction is close and intense. This is a very difficult job and finding the right person with the right personality is worth the wait.

Q. Why do we often see what looks like lack of appreciation on the part of the care recipient?

A. Family members are often looking for the person and personality of the relative that used to exist before the dementia set in. This is natural. A person with dementia, or any other mental illness, certainly looks like the person they once were. However, the patient is gradually losing the ability to recognize and appreciate the care that is given because these social skills have been lost. Don't look for appreciation and you won't be disappointed that it's not there.

Q. Why is there so much suspiciousness and distrust in the dementia patient?

A. Paranoia is often part of the illness. It is to be expected. Even without paranoia, the patient often forgets where he or she put things. Later, unable to find them, the patient turns to the idea of theft, for example, to explain the item's absence.

Q. Why do sibling disagreements so often occur when a parent needs care?
A. This is also common. One sibling always seems to do more for many reasons: financial, proximity, personality and work responsibilities, to name a few. However, all the siblings need to remember that after the parent dies, they may need each other more than ever and that the family needs to continue to exist. Outside counselors can help resolve differences and help the many misunderstandings than can come up when adult children are so stressed about their parent. Give your siblings some decision-making powers, even if they are small, to keep them active and involved in caregiving responsibilities.

Q. How do families know which nursing home is the best for their relative?
A. I always recommend visiting a minimum of three facilities so a comparison can be made among them. Look for accreditation standards, licensing, credentials of administrators and department heads, cleanliness and the general organization of the place. Having the facility within a comfortable distance for visitation is very important for the family members. Asking a professional is important. A gerontologist, geriatric social worker or geriatrician are all good people with whom to consult.

Q. Why is there so much anger in the institutionalized dementia patient? How can families deal with it?
A. There are many reasons for anger. The transition from home to a nursing facility is a hard one. It required relinquishing many familiar things which will not be permitted into the home: a favorite chair, a treasured quilt, a loving companion animal, for example. Dementia itself often distorts the emotions and the depression that frequently goes along with the first several stages of dementia also manifests itself in anger and a lashing-out behavior in the older person. It needs to be

calmly dealt with by the family. A soft, comforting tone of voice reassures the patient that all is being taken care of. Switching to another topic, thereby distracting the patient from the angry thought, also can help. There are also several medications that can be provided which control this type of behavior, when all else fails.

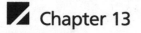 Chapter 13

An Interview with the Author

How many years did you spend investigating elder crime?
I investigated health fraud and patient abuse for the New York State
Attorney General's Medicaid Fraud Control Unit for almost twenty
years. As an investigator, I saw firsthand the tragedies that can occur
when older patients are abused, defrauded or neglected.

What do you recommend to prevent elder crime?
I have warned my family and friends with elder care concerns to be
very careful, to consult with trained health care professionals, to remain
actively involved in every aspect of care and to make frequent unannounced visits to healthcare facilities.

**Can you give an example of the dangers associated with elder
care?**
By far the worst cases of elder abuse I ever saw or heard of, involved
vulnerable patients who were placed in the hands of *illegal and unlicensed* elder care providers. You may wonder what kind of people would
allow older relatives to be placed in an illegal or "underground" nursing home. The answer is: all kinds of people—spouses, adult children,
nieces, nephews and even the patients themselves—all of whom faced

the same dilemma. Medicare did not cover their nursing home care and they were not poor enough to qualify for Medicaid. They had no long-term care insurance and were desperate to preserve a lifetime of savings; under pressure, they used poor judgement. I consider the link between finances and elder abuse the most urgent issue in elder care, which is why the first chapter of *Elder Care* examines this subject in detail.

Have you observed improvements in elder care?

Yes. Many of the nursing homes that were in operation back in the seventies, when I was first hired as an investigator, are no longer in business today. Some of those nursing homes did not meet the higher standards that were imposed by regulatory agencies, while others were closed due to the corrupt practices of their owners. I have observed the emergence of a more patient-friendly nursing homes operated by professional staffs.

Is abuse of the elderly still a problem?

Yes. Although there have been great improvements in the architecture of nursing homes, breakthroughs in medicine and greater emphasis in gerontology, it remains a people business. The elderly remain vulnerable to abuse by their trusted caregivers.

Do you have an elder care website?

Yes. For more information about elder care issues log on to my website: **http://www.eldertips.com**

What is long-term care?

Long-term care is not one service, but many different support services aimed at helping people with chronic conditions. Long-term care patients require the assistance of others to perform the essential activities of daily living (ADL). These activities include eating/feeding, bathing, dressing, transferring (e.g. moving from bed to chair), using the toilet and maintaining continence.

Is long-term care expensive?

Yes! A year at a quality nursing home or three daily shifts of qualified home care workers can easily cost $50,000 per year or more.

Where is long-term care provided?

At home, in an assisted-living residence or in a nursing home.

Does Medicare pay for long-term care?

NO! Medicare does not pay for long-term nursing home or home care for patients who require custodial care.

Does Medicaid pay for long-term care?

Yes. However, Medicaid is the health insurer for the poor. In order to qualify for Medicaid, a patient first has to draw on all of his or her assets, not just income, to pay for long-term care.

Does private insurance cover long-term care?

Yes. To date, though, very few people have purchased long-term care (LTC) insurance which is a fairly new insurance product. As with life insurance, the young and healthy pay a lower premium than the older consumer.

What is a nursing home?

A nursing home is a skilled facility that provides a high level of care to patients. A nursing home provides nursing supervision twenty-four hours a day. A nursing home can provide two types of care, short term rehabilitative care for post-hospitalization recovery and long-term custodial care.

What is an assisted-living facility?

An assisted-living facility is a residence that provides personal assistance, but does not provide medical care or full time nursing supervision. This type of residence is becoming a popular option for seniors throughout the country. Many assisted-living facilities do not participate in Medicare or Medicaid programs, therefore their clients are private payers. Clients, residents or customers are important words in the assisted-living industry, because the residents are not patients. These facilities may provide meals, rooms and other services for their clients, however the amount of additional care they can provide is limited by each state.

Is an assisted-living facility the same as a nursing home?
No. An assisted-living residence does not provide full-time nursing supervision, but does provide some non-medical services including food preparation and activities. Chapter 6 gives a detailed explanation of this type of dependent living arrangement.

Does a client of an assisted-living facility have to sign a contract?
More than likely, yes. Since this is not a highly regulated industry, it is very important for clients to understand their obligations before they sign contracts. I would recommend that they review any admission agreements with the attorneys of their (the client's) choice, before they sign contracts.

Are older patients at risk when they need home care?
Unfortunately for older Americans, home care, in which workers have frequent unsupervised access to vulnerable patients and their property, offers exceptional opportunities and temptations for fraud. The fact that home care workers are often paid low wages for a demanding job that requires significant responsibility, as well as strenuous physical labor, increases the temptations.

How much caution should a person use before hiring a home care worker?
Early planning is especially important in home care. It is important to remember that thieves are proficient at disguising their motives and may appear to be compassionate caregivers when they apply for employment. Hire those from licensed agencies only, and always check references.

How can a consumer prevent home care fraud and abuse?
Before a home care consumer allows a stranger into his or her home, both short- and long-term plans and precautions should be in place. A six-step process, combined with frequent unannounced visits by family and friends can help to protect elders from fraud and abuse.

1. Prepare the Home
A fall can cause a fracture or other injury, making the patient more dependent and vulnerable. There are many practical ways to increase the safety of a home. Remove hazards such as small step-stools, loose rugs, electrical cords and other potential dangers. Provide night-lights near steps and in bathrooms. Phones should be accessible throughout the home so that emergency calls can be made. Bathrooms should be modified to accommodate safety features.

2. Safeguard Possessions
Remove temptations before a home care worker begins employment. All cash, jewelry, financial records, checkbooks and credit cards should be in a protected location such as a safe or a safe-deposit box. Social Security, pension and investment checks should be direct-deposited to prevent theft and forgery. Monitor the mail to make certain that the patient receives his or her routine monthly financial statements listing recent transactions. Don't just throw them in a drawer unread; check all statements for unusual or unauthorized activity. Although there is convenience in electronic banking and credit cards, there is also fraud danger. For example, in one case of elder crime, a man working as a home health care aide for a sixty-eight-year-old male client, was accused of using his patient's credit cards and blank checks to steal $30,000 worth of merchandise and cash. Police said the thefts took place over an eight month period while the aide worked for the disabled man.

3. Install Medical Equipment
Any medical equipment that helps maintain independence is a safe-

guard. Walkers, wheelchairs, hearing aids, eyeglasses and hospital beds are examples. The more active and alert the patient, the less opportunity for abuse or fraud.

4. Screen Potential Home Care Workers

There are many certified home health care agencies that provide home care service. A home care worker can also be hired independently. Screen all applicants with a prepared telephone interview in which you ask for specific information such as licensing, experience and references, and require that an employment application be filled out and submitted. Do not give your address or any other personal information until you have verified the information gathered in the telephone interview. For the most part, checking a reference or license is not a complicated procedure; however, you must do your homework.

5. Take Advantage of Respite Care

Many family caregivers devote themselves so fully to their chronically ill spouse or parent that they neglect their own needs. It is important to take time off from the rigors of caring for an elder family member. Respite care for caregivers is available from visiting nurses, home health aides and other professional home care workers, as well as such sources as senior centers, meals-on-wheels and adult day care centers. The stress relief provided by respite services helps both caregivers and patients. An exhausted caregiver can only provide limited care.

6. Involve Family and Friends

When all other precautions have been taken and a home health care regimen is established, make frequent, unscheduled visits, positioning the home health care worker as part of a *support team*. Encourage other family members and friends to stop by unannounced, as well.

As the headlines attest, using unreliable providers who entice clients and their families with "bargain priced" care can lead to tragedy. But patients and their families can protect themselves from elder fraud and abuse.

 Epilogue

More than twelve million Americans, mostly elderly, need some type of long-term care. This number will increase dramatically when the baby-boom generation enters their retirement years. Long-term care is not one unified program, but many different support services aimed at helping people who have lost some capacity for self-care due to a chronic condition or illness. These patients require the help of others to perform what are referred to as "activities of daily living" (ADL), which include eating/feeding, bathing, dressing, and moving from bed to chair, etc. Such care is expensive and can easily cost a consumer $50,000 per year or more. During my twenty year career as an investigator, I recognized that the financial stress of paying for long-term care, especially when it is an unexpected expense, can result in elderly patients being susceptible to fraud, neglect, and abuse. I also realized that elder crimes are often preventable, which is why I wrote this book.

How are these services paid for? Medicare, the health insurer for older Americans, does not cover long-term custodial care, either in nursing homes or at home. Medicaid does, but has stringent eligibility requirements, including an income and assets "ceiling." Simply put, poverty is a prerequisite for participation in the Medicaid program. This forces many older patients and their families to pay privately for elder care, usually with great financial difficulty and stress. Most older Americans who need long-term care cannot qualify for Medicaid until they have exhausted their life savings. Regrettably, despite the fact that the elder care marketplace offers many attractive options for the senior consumer, not every senior citizen has the financial resources to take advantage of all the available choices. This is unfortunate, since elder care needs are best served when a patient has freedom of choice and can make immediate changes whenever necessary to optimize his or her care.

Over the course of my twenty years "in the field," many senior patients, their families, friends, and caregivers, made a powerful impression on me. Elder care is a demanding job. Although their have been great improvements in the architecture of nursing homes, breakthroughs in medicine, and greater emphasis on gerontology, elder care remains a people business. A strong bond often develops between elder patients and their caregivers. The following story illustrates many of the dilemmas, difficult issues, rewards, and challenges in the real world of elder care.

Joe died at the age of eighty-three, after three serious strokes and a long, courageous battle against cancer, but Joe's challenges had started much earlier. He was born deaf long before the terms 'hearing-impaired' or 'disabled' entered the vernacular. Deafness was characterized as a 'handicap,' but Joe's intelligence, pride, and determination enabled him to live an independent life.

Joe was admitted into a nursing home after he had his first stroke and lost feeling in his right side. He followed his rehabilitation program to the letter and was back home in six weeks.

His second and third strokes were more severe, leaving him completely bedridden and paralyzed on his right side. Joe's doctor had more bad news for him after a series of tests at the hospital. Joe had advanced stomach cancer and would probably live only another few months.

Joe made a conscious decision: he did not want any more operations. Many years before, while he was still healthy, he had discussed his wishes with his attorney, who had prepared both a will and a living will. In addition, on admission to the hospital, Joe had signed a DNR (Do Not Resuscitate) order.

He had to stay in the hospital, being tube-fed, until he could be transferred to a nursing home. Within a day of the transfer, Joe's feeding tube became disconnected. His doctor was able to reconnect the tube in the nursing home without an operation but was concerned that the connection would not last. Many of the caregivers on staff at the nursing home hoped that Joe would reconsider his decision against surgery, but time was running out. Within a few days, Joe's feeding tube again became disconnected, and he refused to go back to the hospital for surgical reinsertion.

The nursing home had on file all of the legal documents necessary to support Joe's decision, but just to make certain that he hadn't changed his mind since signing his advance directives, the staff tried to find an interpreter to speak with him.

The nursing supervisor contacted a local school for the deaf, which immediately sent over an interpreter. However, unbeknownst to the nursing supervisor, there is more than one sign language, and the interpreter "spoke" a different dialect than Joe. Another interpreter was found and rushed to Joe's bedside. It took some time to get Joe to communicate, but he finally answered the question. Speaking in a hushed and somber voice, the interpreter said Joe had told him, "No more operations." The words Joe had actually signed were, "Enough is enough."

Joe's moving story is an example of the positive aspects of an optimal elder care situation and provides many valuable lessons. It reveals just how difficult it is for many caregivers who provide elder care. They often make extraordinary efforts to comfort their patients. Joe's story also stresses the value of using trained caregivers and licensed facilities for elderly patients. The staff at Joe's nursing home could have merely followed their patient's advance directives; this was all they were required to do, and the legalities were all in place. But they went above and beyond the call of duty to give Joe one last chance to change his mind. Joe's story clearly reveals the important differences between a nursing home that simply meets requirements and one that goes above and beyond, providing exceptional care.

The dangers that may be encountered when there are no safeguards in place for choosing trustworthy care for our elderly citizens have been provided throughout *Elder Care*. However, as the compassionate and caring treatment Joe found clearly shows, tragic cases of theft, fraud, and abuse of elderly patients do not have to happen to any seniors. By following the guidelines and advice in *Elder Care*, doing individual research, and using care and vigilance, seniors and their families can take the necessary steps towards protecting themselves and those they love and make Joe's example of exceptional care a reality.

 **Afterword**

I would like to end this book with the words of President John Fitz-gerald Kennedy from his last speech, a speech that JFK was to deliver at a luncheon at the Dallas Trade Mart on November 22, 1963. He was assassinated only minutes before his scheduled talk.

"...WE IN THIS COUNTRY, IN THIS GENERATION, ARE BY DESTINY, RATHER THAN BY CHOICE—THE WATCHMEN..."

We, you and I, must be worthy of the responsibility entrusted to us by our elders.

We must be the Watchmen!!

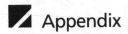 **Appendix**

Elder Care Locator

The Elder Care Locator is a service of the United States Department of Health and Human Services, Administration of Aging. This service is designed to put you in touch with state and local resources available to assist the older American in need. The service is available Monday through Friday at 1-800-677-1116.

The Administration on Aging

Department of Health & Human Services
200 Independence Avenue, S.W. / Washington, DC 20201
Phone: (202) 619-0724 / Fax: (202) 619-3759
toll-free: (800) 677-1116
e-mail: aoainfo@ban-gate.aoa.dhhs.gov
http://www.aoa.gov

The Administration on Aging is the federal focal point and advocacy agency for senior Americans. Their web site provides hundreds of valuable resources for seniors and their families, including *The Resource Directory for Older People*. This Directory is a cooperative effort of the National Institute on Aging (NIA) and the Administration on Aging (AoA).

The Offices of Aging

The Office of Aging provides valuable resources to patients and families in crisis. Often your local county or city maintains an Office of Aging. I have been to my local county Office of Aging and found numerous referrals for elder care services, as well as information on senior citizen services. I found that in addition to the usual office personnel, there were several "seasoned citizens" who were genuinely interested in helping clients with any elder-related issues.

Following is a list of the addresses and phone numbers of each state's Office of Aging. This department will provide you with resources and information, as well as the address of your local city or county office.

Alabama

Commission of Aging / RSA Plaza, Ste. 470 / 770 Washington Ave. / Montgomery, AL 36130 / Phone: (334) 242-5743 Fax: (334) 242-5594

Alaska

Alaska Commission on Aging / Dept. of Admin. / P.O. Box 110209 / Juneau, AK 99811-0209 / Phone: (907) 465-3250 Fax: (907) 465-4716

Arizona

Aging & Adult Administration / Dept. of Economic Security / 1789 W. Jefferson / Phoenix, AZ 85007 Phone: (602) 542-4446

Arkansas

Aging & Adult Svcs. / P.O. Box 1437 / Little Rock, AR 72203 / Phone: (501) 682-8521 Fax: (501) 682-8155

California

Dept. of Aging / 1600 K St. / Sacramento, CA 95814 / Phone: (916) 322-5290

Colorado
Aging & Adult Svcs. Div. / Dept. of Human Svcs. / 110 16th St., 2nd
Fl. / Denver, CO 80203 / Phone: (303) 620-4127 Fax: (303) 620-4189

Connecticut
Commission on Aging / 25 Sigourney St., 8th Fl. / Hartford, CT
06106-5003 / Phone: (203) 424-5360

Delaware
Div. of Aging Health & Social Svcs. Dept. / 1901 N. DuPont Hwy. /
New Castle, DE 19720 / Phone: (302) 577-4660 Fax: (302) 577-4793

Florida
Dept. of Elder Affairs / 1317 Winewood Blvd. / Bldg. E, Rm. 317 /
Tallahassee, FL 32399-0700 / Phone: (904) 922-5297 Fax: (904) 922-
6216

Georgia
Div. of Aging / Dept. of Human Resources / 2 Peachtree St., #18 /
Atlanta, GA 30303 / Phone: (404) 657-5255

Hawaii
Executive Off. on Aging / 335 Merchant St., Rm. 241 / Honolulu, HI
96813 / Phone: (808) 586-0100 Fax: (808) 586-0185

Idaho
Off. on Aging / Statehouse, Rm. 108 / Boise, ID 83703 / Phone: (208)
334-3833

Illinois
Dept. on Aging / 421 E. Capitol / Springfield, IL 62701 / Phone: (217)
785-2870 Fax: (217) 785-4477

Iowa

Dept. of Elder Affairs / 914 Grand, 2nd Fl. / Des Moines, IA 50309 /
Phone: (515) 281-5188 Fax: (515) 281-4036

Kansas

Dept. of Aging / Docking State Off. Bldg., Rm. 150-S / Topeka, KS
66612-1500 / Phone: (913) 296-4986 Fax: (913) 296-0256

Kentucky

Div. of Aging Services / Dept. for Social Svcs. / 2275 E. Main St. /
Frankfort, KY 40621 / Phone: (502) 564-6930

Louisiana

Off. of Elderly Affairs / 4550 North Blvd. Baton Rouge, LA 70806 /
Phone: (504) 925-1700

Maine

Bur. of Elder & Adult Services / Dept. of Human Svcs. / State House
Station #11 / Augusta, ME 04333 Phone: (207) 624-5335

Maryland

Off. on Aging / 301 W. Preston St., Rm. 1004 / Baltimore, MD 21201 /
Phone: (410) 225-1102 Fax: (410) 333-7943

Massachusetts

Executive Office of Elder Affairs / 1 Ashburton Pl., 5th Fl. / Boston,
MA 02108 / Phone: (617) 727-7750

Michigan

Off. of Services on Aging / 611 W. Ottawa St., 3rd Fl. / Lansing, MI
48909 / Phone: (517) 373-8230 Fax: (517) 373-4092

Minnesota
Board on Aging / Human Svcs. Bldg., 4th Fl. / 444 Lafayette Rd. / St.
Paul, MN 55155 / Phone: (612) 296-2770

Mississippi
Director / Council on Aging / Dept. of Human Svcs. / P.O. Box 352 /
Jackson, MS 39205-0352

Missouri
Div. of Aging / Dept. of Social Svcs. / P.O. Box 1337 / Jefferson City,
MO 65102 / Phone: (314) 751-8535 Fax: (314) 751-8687

Montana
Aging Division / Dept. of Family Svcs. / 48 N. Last Chance Gulch /
Helena, MT 59604 / Phone: (406) 444-5900

Nebraska
Dept. on Aging / 301 Centennial Mall S. / P.O. Box 95044 / Lincoln,
NE 68509-5044 / Phone: (402) 471-2306 Fax: (402) 471-4619

Nevada
Div. for Aging Svcs. / 340 N. 11th St., Ste. 114 / Las Vegas, NV 89101 /
Phone: (702) 486-3545

New Hampshire
Div. of Elderly Svcs. / Dept. of Health & Human Svcs. / 115 Pleasant
St., Annex Bldg. 1 / Concord, NH 03301 / Phone: (603) 271-2751

New Jersey
Div. on Aging / Dept. of Community Affairs / 101 S. Broad St., CN807 /
Trenton, NJ 08625 / Phone: (609) 292-4833 (800) 792-8820

New Mexico

State Agency on Aging / 228 E. Palace Ave. / Santa Fe, NM 87501/
Phone: (505) 827-7640 Fax: (505) 827-7649

New York

Off. of the Aging / Agency Bldg. 2 / Empire State Plaza / Albany, NY
12223 / Phone: (518) 474-4425

North Carolina

Aging Div. / Dept. of Human Resources / 101 Blair Dr. / Raleigh,
NC 27603 / Phone: (919) 733-3983 Fax: (919) 715-4645

North Dakota

Aging Svcs. Div. / Dept. of Human Svcs. / P.O. Box 7070 / Bismarck,
ND 58507-7070 / Phone: (701) 328-2577 Fax: (701) 328-5466

Ohio

Comm. on Aging / Dept. of Aging / 50 W. Broad St., 9th Fl. /
Columbus, OH 43266 / Phone: (614) 466-7246 Fax: (614) 466-5741

Oklahoma

Dept. of Human Svcs. / P.O. Box 25352 / Oklahoma City, OK 73125 /
Phone: (405) 521-2778

Oregon

Senior & Disabled Svc. / Dept. of Human Resources / 500 Summer
St., NE / Salem, OR 97310-1015 / Phone: (503) 945-5810 Fax: (503)
373-7823

Pennsylvania

Dept. of Aging / Market St. Off. Bldg., 7th Fl. / Harrisburg, PA 17120 /
Phone: (717) 783-1550

Rhode Island
Dept. of Elderly Affairs / 160 Pine St. / Providence, RI 02903 / Phone:
(401) 277-2894 Fax: (401) 277-1490

South Carolina
Div. on Aging / 202 Arbor Lake Dr. / Columbia, SC 29223 / Phone:
(803) 737-7500

South Dakota
Div. of Adult Svcs. & Aging / Dept. of Social Svcs. / Kneip Bldg. /
Pierre, SD 57501 / Phone: (605) 773-3165

Tennessee
Comm. on Aging / 706 Church St. / Nashville, TN 37243 / Phone:
(615) 741-2056

Texas
Dept. on Aging / P.O. Box 12786, Capitol Station / Austin, TX 78711 /
Phone: (512) 444-2727

Utah
Div. of Aging / Dept. of Social Svcs. / 120 N. 200 W., Rm. 401 / Salt
Lake City, UT 84103 / Phone: (801) 538-3918

Vermont
Dept. of Aging & Disabilities / Human Svcs. Agcy. / 103 S. Main St. /
Waterbury, VT 05671 / Phone: (802) 241-2400 Fax: (802) 241-2325

Virginia
Dept. for the Aging / 700 E. Franklin St., 10th Fl. / Richmond, VA
23219 / Phone: (804) 225-2271

Washington
Aging & Adult Svcs. Admin. / Dept. of Social & Health Svcs. / P.O.
Box 45050 / Olympia, WA 98504 / Phone: (360) 586-3768

West Virginia
Comm. on Aging / Holly Grove / 1710 Kanawha Blvd. E. / Charleston,
WV 25311 / Phone: (304) 558-3317 Fax: (304) 558-0004

Wisconsin
- Board on Aging & Long Term Care / 214 N. Hamilton, 2nd Fl. /
Madison, WI 53702 / Phone: (608) 266-8944
- Bureau on Aging / Dept. of Health & Social Services / P.O. Box 7851 /
Madison, WI 53707 / Phone: (608) 266-1345 Fax: (608) 266-7882

Wyoming
Div. on Aging / Dept. of Health / 139 Hathaway Bldg. / Cheyenne,
WY 82002 / Phone: (307) 777-7986

District of Columbia
Off. on Aging / 441 4th St., NW, 9th Fl. / Washington, DC 20001-
2700 / Phone: (202) 724-5622

American Samoa
Territorial Admin. on Aging / American Samoa Government / Pago
Pago, AS 96799 / Phone: (684) 633-1251 Fax: (684) 633-7723

Guam
Dept. of Public Health & Social Svcs. / P.O. Box 2816 / Agana, GU
96910 / Phone: (671) 734-7399

Northern Mariana Islands
Aging Off. Community & Cultural Affairs / Lower Base / Saipan, MP
96950 / Phone: (670) 234-6696 Fax: (670) 234-2565

Puerto Rico
Gericulture Comm. / P.O. Box 50063 / Old San Juan, PR 00910 /
Phone: (809) 721-5710 Fax: (809) 721-6510

U.S. Virgin Islands
Dept. of Human Svcs. / 20 A Strand St. & 5BB Smith St. Christiansted /
St. Croix, VI 00820 / Phone: (809) 774-0930

State Attorney General's Office
I have worked as an investigator for the New York State Attorney
General's Office for more than nineteen years. Most states have a
Medicaid Fraud Control Unit within the Attorney General's Office
which concentrates on many health fraud and elder care issues. In addition, the Attorney General's Office has other investigative divisions
relating to consumer fraud and other violations. If you encounter a
questionable practice by an elder care provider, contact the Attorney
General's Office in your state using the following list of addresses and
phone numbers or refer to the web site that follows this list for more
information.

Alabama
Office of the Attorney General / 11 S. Union St. / Montgomery, AL
36130 / Phone: (334) 242-7300 Fax: (334) 242-7458

Alaska
Attorney General / P.O. Box 110300 / Diamond Courthouse / Juneau,
AK 99811-0300 / Phone: (907) 465-3600 Fax: (907) 465-2075

Arizona
Attorney General / 1275 W. Washington St. / Phoenix, AZ 85007 /
Phone: (602) 542-4266

Arkansas

Attorney General / 200 Tower Bldg. / 323 Center St., Ste. 200 / Little Rock, AR 72201-2610 / Phone: (501) 682-2007 Fax: (501) 682-8084

California

Attorney General / 1300 I Street, Suite 1740 / Sacramento, CA 95814 / Phone: (916) 324-5437

Colorado

Attorney General / Dept. of Law / 1525 Sherman St. / Denver, CO 80203 / Phone: (303) 866-3052 Fax: (303) 866-5691

Connecticut

Attorney General / 55 Elm St. / Hartford, CT 06141-0120 / Phone: (860) 808-5318

Delaware

Attorney General / Carvel State Office Bldg. / 820 N. French St. / Wilmington, DE 19801 / Phone: (302) 577-8400 Fax: (302) 577-3090

Florida

Attorney General / The Capital, PL 01 / Tallahassee, FL 32399-1050 / Phone: (850) 487-1963 Fax: (850) 487-2564

Georgia

Office of the Attorney General / 40 Capital Square, S.W. / Atlanta, GA 30334-1300 / Phone: (404) 656-4585

Hawaii

Attorney General / 425 Queen St. / Honolulu, HI 96813 / Phone: (808) 586-1282 Fax: (808) 586-1239

Idaho

Attorney General of Idaho / Statehouse / Boise, ID 83720-1000 / Phone: (208) 334-2400

Illinois

Attorney General / 100 W. Randolph St. / Chicago, IL 60601 / Phone: (312) 814-2503 Fax: (312) 814-2549

Indiana

Office of the Attorney General / 402 W. Washington St., 5th Fl. / Indianapolis, IN 46204 / Phone: (317) 233-4386

Iowa

Attorney General of Iowa / Hoover State Off. Bldg. / Des Moines, IA 50319 / Phone: (515) 281-3053 Fax: (515) 281-3604

Kansas

Attorney General / Judicial Bldg. / 301 W. Tenth St. / Topeka, KS 66612-1597 / Phone: (785) 296-2215 Fax: (785) 296-6296

Kentucky

Office of the Attorney General / State Capital, Rm. 116 / Frankfort, KY 40601 / Phone: (502) 564-7600

Louisiana

Attorney General / Department of Justice / P.O. Box 94095 / Baton Rouge, LA 70804-4095 / Phone: (225) 342-7013

Maine

Attorney General / State House Station Six / Augusta, ME 04333 / Phone: (207) 626-8800

Maryland
Attorney General / 200 Saint Paul Place / Baltimore, MD 21202-2202 / Phone: (410) 576-6300 Fax: (410) 576-7003

Massachusetts
Attorney General / One Ashburton Pl. / Boston, MA 02108-1698 / Phone: (617) 727-2200 Fax: (617) 727-3251

Michigan
Attorney General / P.O. Box 30212 / 525 W. Ottawa St. / Lansing, MI 48909-0212 / Phone: (517) 373-1110

Minnesota
Office of the Attorney General / State Capitol, Suite 102 / St. Paul, MN 55155 / Phone: (651) 296-6196

Mississippi
Attorney General / Department of Justice / P.O. Box 220 / Jackson, MS 39205-0220 / Phone: (601) 359-3692

Missouri
Attorney General / Supreme Court Bldg. / 207 W. High St. / Jefferson City, MO 65101 / Phone: (573) 751-3321 Fax: (573) 751-0774

Montana
Attorney General / Justice Building / 215 N. Sanders St. / Helena, MT 59620-1401 / Phone: (406) 444-2026

Nebraska
Attorney General / P.O. Box 98920 / Lincoln, NE 68509-8920 / Phone: (402) 471-2682 Fax: (402) 471-3297

Nevada
Attorney General / Old Supreme Court Building / 100 N. Carson St. / Carson City, NV 89710 / Phone: (775) 687-4170

New Hampshire
Office of the Attorney General / State House Annex / 25 Capitol St. / Concord, NH 03301-6397 / Phone: (603) 271-3658

New Jersey
Attorney General / Hughes Justice Complex / 25 Market St., CN080 / Trenton, NJ 08625 / Phone: (609) 292-4925

New Mexico
Attorney General / P.O. Drawer 1508 / Santa Fe, NM 87504-1508 / Phone: (505) 827-6000 Fax: (505) 827-5826

New York
Attorney General / Dept. of Law / The Capitol, 2nd Floor / Albany, NY 12224 / Phone: (518) 474-7330

North Carolina
Attorney General / P.O. Box 629 / Raleigh, NC 27602-0629 / Phone: (919) 716-6400

North Dakota
Attorney General / State Capitol, 1st Fl. / 600 E. Boulevard Ave. / Bismarck, ND 58505-0040 / Phone: (701) 328-2210 Fax: (701) 328-2226

Ohio
Office of the Attorney General / State Office Tower / 30 E. Broad St. / Columbus, OH 43266-0410 / Phone: (614) 466-3376

Oklahoma
Attorney General / State Capitol / 2300 N. Lincoln Blvd., Rm. 112 / Oklahoma City, OK 73105 / Phone: (405) 521-3921

Oregon
Attorney General / Justice Building / 1162 Court St., NE / Salem, OR 97310 / Phone: (503) 378-6002

Pennsylvania
Attorney General / Strawberry Square / Harrisburg, PA 17120 / Phone: (717) 787-3391

Rhode Island
Attorney General / 150 S. Main St. / Providence, RI 02903 / Phone: (401) 274-4400

South Carolina
Attorney General / Rembert C. Dennis Office Bldg. / P.O. Box 11549 / Columbia, SC 29211-1549 / Phone: (803) 734-3970

South Dakota
Attorney General / Office of the Attorney General / 500 E. Capitol / Pierre, SD 57501-5070 / Phone: (605) 773-3215

Tennessee
Attorney General / 500 Charlotte Ave. / Nashville, TN 37243 / Phone: (615) 741-6474

Texas
Attorney General / Capitol Station / P.O. Box 12548 / Austin, TX 78711-2548 / Phone: (512) 463-2191

Utah
Attorney General / 236 State Capitol, Rm. 236 / Salt Lake City, UT 84114-0810 / Phone: (801) 538-1326

Vermont
Attorney General / 109 State St. / Montpelier, VT 05609-1001 / Phone: (802) 828-3171 Fax: (802) 828-2154

Virginia
Attorney General / Supreme Court Bldg. / 900 E. Main St. / Richmond, VA 23219 / Phone: (804) 786-2071 Fax: (804) 371-0200

Washington
Office of the Attorney General / P.O. Box 40100 / 1125 Washington St., SE / Olympia, WA 98504-0100 / Phone: (360) 753-6200

West Virginia
Office of the Attorney General / State Capitol / 1900 Kanawha Blvd, East / Charleston, WV 25305 / Phone: (304) 558-2021 Fax: (304) 558-0140

Wisconsin
Office of the Attorney General / P.O. Box 7857 / Madison, WI 53305 / Phone: (304) 558-2021

Wyoming
Office of the Attorney General / State Capitol Building / Cheyenne, WY 82002 / Phone: (307) 777-7841

District of Columbia
Office of the Corporation Counsel / 441 4th St., NW / Washington, DC 20001 / Phone: (202) 727-6248

American Samoa
Office of the Attorney General / American Samoa Government / P.O.
Box 7 / Pago Pago, AS 96799 / Phone: (684) 633-4163 Fax: (684) 633-1838

Guam
Attorney General / Judicial Center Bldg. / 120 West O'Brien Drive /
Agana, GU 96910 / Phone: (671) 475-3324

Northern Mariana Islands
Office of the Attorney General / Administration Bldg. / Saipan, MP
96950 / Phone: (670) 664-2341

Puerto Rico
Office of the Attorney General / P.O. Box 192 / San Juan, PR 00902-0192 / Phone: (787) 721-7700 Fax: (787) 724-4770

U.S. Virgin Islands
Attorney General / Dept. of Justice / G.E.R.S. Complex / 48B-50C
Kronprinsden Gade / St. Thomas, VI 00802 / Phone: (809) 774-5666
Fax: (809) 774-9710

The National Association of Attorneys General (NAAG)
http://www.naag.org
The National Association of Attorneys General web site provides information on many fraud and consumer issues and links to every state attorney general's web site. It also provides a full listing of each individual states' attorney general's office including address, phone and fax number.

The State Health Department

The state health department enforces the public health laws and administers health programs and services in each state. The health department may issue inspection and other types of reports, which are available to the public. This information can assist you in choosing a particular nursing home or assisted living residence. In addition, patients or visitors to a facility can file a complaint with the health department regarding a problem with the premises, the food or the condition of the patients.

Alabama
State Public Health Dept. / 610 E. Patton / Montgomery, AL 36111 / Phone: (334) 613-5200 Fax: (334) 240-3387

Alaska
Div. of Public Health / P.O. Box 110610 / Juneau, AK 99811-0610 / Phone: (907) 465-3090 Fax: (907) 586-1877

Arizona
Dept. of Health Services / 1740 W. Adams St. / Phoenix, AZ 85007 / Phone: (602) 542-1025

Arkansas
Dept. of Health / 4815 W. Markham St. / Little Rock, AR 72205 / Phone: (501) 661-2417 Fax: (501) 661-2601

California
Dept. of Health Services / 714 P Street, Rm. 1253 / Sacramento, CA 95814 / Phone: (916) 657-1425

Colorado
Dept. of Public Health & Environment / 4300 Cherry Cheek Dr., S. / Denver, CO 80222 / Phone: (303) 692-2100 Fax: (303) 782-0095

Connecticut
Dept. of Public Health / Dept. of Health Services / 150 Washington St. / Hartford, CT 06106 / Phone: (203) 566-2038

Delaware
Div. of Public Health / Dept. of Health & Social Svcs. / P.O. Box 637 / Dover, DE 19903 / Phone: (302) 739-4701 Fax: (302) 739-6659

Florida
Dept. of Health & Rehab. Svcs. / 1317 Winewood Blvd. / Tallahassee, FL 32399-0700 / Phone: (904) 487-2705 Fax: (904) 922-2993

Georgia
Public Health Div. / Dept. of Human Resources / 2 Peachtree St., 7th Fl. / Atlanta, GA 30303 / Phone: (404) 657-2702

Hawaii
Dept. of Health / P.O. Box 3378 / Honolulu, HI 96801 / Phone: (808) 586-4410 Fax: (808) 586-4444

Idaho
Idaho Dept. of Health & Welfare / 450 W. State St., 10th Fl. / P.O. Box 83720 / Boise, ID 83720-0036 / Phone: (208) 334-5500

Illinois
Dept. of Public Health / 535 W. Jefferson St. / Springfield, IL 62761 / Phone: (217) 782-4977 Fax: (217) 782-3987

Indiana
State Board of Health / 1330 West Michigan Street, #4255 / Indianapolis, IN 46206 / Phone: (317) 383-6100

Iowa
Dept. of Public Health / Lucas State Off. Bldg. / Des Moines, IA 50319 /
Phone: (515) 281-5605 Fax: (515) 281-4958

Kansas
Dept. of Health & Environment / Landon State Off. Bldg., 6th Fl. /
Topeka, KS 66612-1290 / Phone: (913) 296-1500 Fax: (913) 296-1231

Kentucky
Dept. for Health Services / Cabinet for Human Resources / 275 E.
Main St. / Frankfort, KY 40601 Phone: (502) 564-3970

Louisiana
Dept. of Health & Hospitals / P.O. Box 3214 / Baton Rouge, LA 70821 /
Phone: (504) 342-8092

Maine
Dept. of Human Services / State House Station #11 / Augusta, ME
04333 / Phone: (207) 287-2736

Maryland
Dept. of Health & Mental Hygiene / 201 W. Preston St., 5th Fl. /
Baltimore, MD 21201 / Phone: (410) 225-6505

Massachusetts
Dept. of Public Health / 150 Tremont St. / Boston, MA 02111 / Phone:
(617) 727-0201

Michigan
Dept. of Public Health / 3500 N. Logan / P.O. Box 30035 / Lansing,
MI 48909 / Phone: (517) 335-8024 Fax: (517) 335-9476

Minnesota
Dept. of Health / 717 Delaware St., SE / P.O. Box 9441 / Minneapolis,
MN 55400 / Phone: (612) 623-5460

Mississippi
Dept. of Health / 2423 N. State St. / Jackson, MS 39216 / Phone: (601)
960-7634

Missouri
Dept. of Health / 1738 E. Elm / P.O. Box 570 / Jefferson City, MO
65102 / Phone: (314) 751-6001 Fax: (314) 751-6041

Montana
Health Services Div. / Dept. of Health & Env. Science / Cogswell Bldg.
Helena, MT 59620 / Phone: (406) 444-4473

Nebraska
Director / Dept. of Health / P.O. Box 95007 / Lincoln, NE 68509 /
Phone: (402) 471-2133

Nevada
Health Div. / Dept. of Human Resources / 505 E. King St., Rm. 201
/ Carson City, NV 89710 / Phone: (702) 687-4740

New Hampshire
Div. of Public Health / Dept. of Health & Human Svcs. / 115 Pleasant
St., Annex Bldg. 1 / Concord, NH 03301 / Phone: (603) 271-4505

New Jersey
Dept. of Health / John Fitch Plz., CN360 / Trenton, NJ 08625 / Phone:
(609) 292-4010

New Mexico
Dept. of Health / 1190 St. Francis Dr. / Santa Fe, NM 87502 / Phone: (505) 827-2613 Fax: (505) 827-2530

New York
Dept. of Health / Corning Tower / Empire State Plz. / Albany, NY 12237 / Phone: (518) 474-2011

North Carolina
Adult Health Promotion / Dept. of Health / 1330 St. Mary's St. / Raleigh, NC 27611-7687 / Phone: (919) 715-3158 Fax: (919) 715-3144

North Dakota
Dept. of Health / 600 E. Boulevard Ave. / Bismarck, ND 58505 / Phone: (701) 328-2372 Fax: (701) 328-4727

Ohio
Dept. of Health / P.O. Box 118 / Columbus, OH 43266-0118 / Phone: (614) 466-2253 Fax: (614) 644-0085

Oklahoma
Dept. of Health / P.O. Box 53551 / Oklahoma City, OK 73152 / Phone: (405) 271-4200

Oregon
Health Division / Dept. of Human Resources / 800 N.E. Oregon St., #21 / Portland, OR 97232 / Phone: (503) 731-4000 Fax: (503) 731-4078

Pennsylvania
Dept. of Health / Health & Welfare Bldg., Rm. 802 / Harrisburg, PA 17120 / Phone: (717) 787-6436

Rhode Island
Dept. of Health / 3 Capital Hill / Providence, RI 02908 / Phone: (401)
277-2231

South Carolina
Health & Environmental Control / 2600 Bull St. / Columbia, SC
29201 / Phone: (803) 734-4880

South Dakota
Dept. of Health / 445 E. Capitol Ave. / Pierre, SD 57501 / Phone:
(605) 773-3361

Tennessee
Dept. of Health / Tennessee Towers, 9th Fl. / Nashville, TN 37247 /
Phone: (615) 741-3111 Fax: (615) 741-2491

Texas
Dept. of Health / 1100 W. 49th St. / Austin, TX 78756 / Phone: (512)
458-7111

Utah
- Div. of Health Care Financing / Dept. of Health / 288 N. 1460 W. /
Salt Lake City, UT 84116 / Phone: (801) 538-6111
- Government & Community Relations / P.O. Box 16700 / Salt Lake
City, UT 84116/ Phone: (801) 538-6332

Vermont
Dept. of Health / 108 Cherry St. / P.O. Box 70 / Burlington, VT 05402 /
Phone: (802) 863-7280 Fax: (802) 863-7425

Virginia
Dept. of Health / Main St. Station / 1500 E. Main St., Rm. 214 /
Richmond, VA 23219 / Phone: (804) 786-3561 Fax: (804) 786-4616

Washington
Dept. of Health / P.O. Box 47800 / Olympia, WA 98504-7800 / Phone: (360) 586-5846

West Virginia
Dept. of Health & Human Resources / State Capitol Complex / Bldg. 3, Rm. 206 / Charleston, WV 25305 / Phone: (304) 558-0684

Wisconsin
Div. of Health / Dept. of Health & Soc. Svcs. / 1 W. Wilson St. / Madison, WI 53702 / Phone: (608) 266-1511 Fax: (608) 267-2832

Wyoming
Dept. of Health / Hathaway Bldg. / Cheyenne, WY 82002 / Phone: (307) 777-7656

District of Columbia
Comm. of Public Health / Dept. of Human Services / 1660 L St., NW, 12th Fl. / Washington, DC 20036 / Phone: (202) 673-7700

American Samoa
Dept. of Health / Pago Pago, AS 96799 / Phone: (684) 633-1222 Fax: (684) 633-1869

Guam
Dept. of Public Health & Social Services / P.O. Box 2816 / Agana, GU 96910 / Phone: (671) 734-7102 Fax: (671) 734-5910

Northern Mariana Islands
Director / Dept. of Public Health & Environmental Svcs. / P.O. Box 409 / Saipan, MP 96950 / Phone: (670) 234-8950

Puerto Rico
Dept. of Health / P.O. Box 70184 / San Juan, PR 00936-0184 / Phone:
(809) 766-1616 Fax: (809) 250-6547

U.S. Virgin Islands
Dept. of Health / St. Thomas Hospital / 48 Sugar Estate / St. Thomas,
VI 00802 / Phone: (809) 776-8311 Fax: (809) 777-4001

The State Department of Licensing
The State Department of Licensing regulates and licenses various professions in the state. The listing of these departments by individual state
is to assist you in verifying the credentials, certifications and licenses of
dependent care facilities, home care employees, agencies and professionals. There are several states that do not have a centralized department of licensing and each profession is regulated by an autonomous
board. I would suggest that if your state does not appear on this list,
you contact the health department for a referral to the appropriate regulatory agency. In addition, the centralized department of licenses might
not regulate all professions. However, a representative should be able to
refer you to the appropriate regulatory agency.

Alaska
Div. of Occupational Licensing / Dept. of Commerce & Economic
Development / P.O. Box 110806 / Juneau, AK 99811-0806 / Phone:
(907) 465-2538 Fax: (907) 465-2974

California
Dept. of Consumer Affairs / 400 R St., Rm. 1060 / Sacramento, CA
95814-6213 / Phone: (916) 445-4465

Colorado
Dept. of Regulatory Agencies / 1560 Broadway, #1550 / Denver, CO
80203 / Phone: (303) 894-7855

Connecticut

Consumer Protection / Bureau of Licensing and Regulation / 165 Capitol Ave. / Hartford, CT 06106 / Phone: (203) 566-4999

Delaware

Div. of Professional Reg. / Dept. of Administrative Svcs. / P.O. Box 1401 / Dover, DE 19903 / Phone: (302) 739-4522 Fax: (302) 739-2711

Florida

- Dept. of Business & Professional Regulation / 1940 N. Monroe St. #60 / Tallahassee, FL 32399-0750 / Phone: (904) 488-2252 Fax: (904) 487-9622
- Div. of Licensing / Dept. of State / Crossland Bldg., 2520 N. Monroe St. / Tallahassee, FL 32303 / Phone: (904) 488-6982

Georgia

State Examining Board / Off. of Secretary of State / 166 Pryor St., SW / Atlanta, GA 30303 / Phone: (404) 656-3900

Hawaii

Dept. of Commerce & Consumer Affairs / 1010 Richards St. / Honolulu, HI 96813 / Phone: (808) 586-2850

Idaho

Occupational Licenses / 1109 Main St., Ste. 220 / Boise, ID 83702-5642 / Phone: (208) 334-3233

Illinois

Dept. of Professional Regulation / 320 Washington St., 3rd Fl. / Springfield, IL 62786 / Phone: (217) 785-0822 Fax: (217) 782-7645

Indiana
- Professional Licensing Agency / 302 W. Washington St., #306 /
Indianapolis, IN 46204 / Phone: (317) 232-3997
- Health Professions Bur. / One American Sq., Rm. 041 / 402 W.
Washington St. / Indianapolis, IN 46204 / Phone: (317) 232-2960

Iowa
Professional Lic. & Regs. Div. / Dept. of Commerce, 1918 SE Hulsizer /
Ankeny, IA 50021 / Phone: (515) 281-5602

Kansas
State Board of Tech. Professions / Landon State Off. Bldg., Ste. 507 /
Topeka, KS 66612-1257 / Phone: (913) 296-3053

Kentucky
Occupations & Professions Div. / Dept. of Admin. / P.O. Box 456 /
Frankfort, KY 40602 / Phone: (502) 564-3296

Louisiana
Off. of Licensing & Regulation / Health & Human Resources Dept. /
P.O. Box 3767 / Baton Rouge, LA 70821 / Phone: (504) 342-0138

Maine
Division of Licensing & Enforcement / Dept. of Prof. & Fin. Reg. /
State House Station #35 / Augusta, ME 04333 / Phone: (207) 582-
8723

Maryland
Dept. of Licensing & Regulation / 501 St. Paul Pl. / Baltimore, MD
21202-2272 / Phone: (301) 333-6200

Massachusetts
Division of Registration / Executive Off. of Consumer Affairs / 100 Cambridge St., Rm. 1520 / Boston, MA 02202 / Phone: (617) 727-3074

Michigan
Department of Licensing & Registration / P.O. Box 30018 / Lansing, MI 48909 / Phone: (517) 373-1870

Minnesota
Enforcement & Licensing Dept. of Commerce / 133 E. 7th St. / St. Paul, MN 55101 / Phone: (612) 296-3528

Mississippi
Secretary of State / P.O. Box 136 / Jackson, MS 39201 / Phone: (601) 359-1350

Missouri
Division of Professional Registration / Dept. of Economic Development / 3605 Missouri Blvd., Box 1335 / Jefferson City, MO 65102 / Phone: (314) 751-1081 Fax: (314) 751-4176

Montana
Professional & Occupational Licensing Bureau / Dept. of Commerce / 111 N. Jackson, Lower Level / Helena, MT 59620 / Phone: (406) 444-3737

Nebraska
Bureau of Examining Bd. / Dept. of Health / P.O. Box 95007 / Lincoln, NE 68509-5007 / Phone: (402) 471-2115

New Hampshire
Secretary of State / 204 State House / Concord, NH 03301 / Phone: (603) 271-3242

New Jersey
Div. of Consumer Affairs / Dept. of Law & Public Safety / P.O. Box 45027 / Newark, NJ 07101 / Phone: (201) 504-6200

New Mexico
Dept. of Regulation & Licensing / P.O. Box 25101 / Santa Fe, NM 87504 / Phone: (505) 827-7199 Fax: (505) 827-7083

New York
- Dept. of State / 162 Washington Ave. / Albany, NY 12231 / Phone: (518) 474-0050
- State Board for Professions / Dept. of State Ed. / Cultural Educ. Cntr., Rm. 3059A / Albany, NY 12230 / Phone: (518) 486-1765

North Dakota
Secretary of State / State Capitol, 1st Floor / 600 E Boulevard Ave / Bismarck, ND 58505-0500 / Phone: (701) 328-2905 Fax: (701) 328-2992

Pennsylvania
Professional & Occupational. Affairs / Dept. of State / 124 Pine St. / Harrisburg, PA 17101 / Phone: (717) 783-7194

Rhode Island
Professional Regulation / Dept. of Health / 75 Davis St. / Providence, RI 02908 / Phone: (401) 277-2827

South Carolina
Dept. of Labor, Licensing & Regulations / P.O. Box 11329 / Columbia, SC 29211 / Phone: (803) 734-9600

South Dakota
Prof. & Occuptional Licensing / Commerce & Regulations Dept. / 910 E. Sioux Ave. / Pierre, SD 57501 / Phone: (605) 773-3178

Tennessee
- Regulatory Boards / Dept. of Commerce & Insurance / Volunteer Plaza, 500 James Robertson Pkwy. / Nashville, TN 37243-0572 / Phone: (615) 741-3449
- Health Related Boards / 287 Plus Park Blvd. / Nashville, TN 37217 / Phone: (615) 367-6220

Texas
Dept. of Licensing & Regulation / P.O. Box 12157 / Austin, TX 78711 / Phone: (512) 463-3173

Utah
Div. of Occupational & Professional Licensing / 160 E. 300 S. / Salt Lake City, UT 84116 / Phone: (801) 530-6620

Vermont
Off. of Professional Reg. / Off. of the Secretary of State / 29 Terrace St. / P.O. Drawer 9 / Montpelier, VT 05609-1106 / Phone: (802) 828-2363 Fax: (802) 828-2496

Virginia
Dept. of Prof. & Occupational Regulation / 3600 W. Broad St. / Richmond, VA 23230 / Phone: (804) 367-8519 Fax: (804) 367-9537

Washington
Dept. of Licensing / Highways-Licensing Bldg. / P.O. Box 9020 / Olympia, WA 98504-9020 / Phone: (360) 902-3600

Wisconsin
Regulation & Licensing Dept. / P.O. Box 8935 / Madison, WI 53708-8935 / Phone: (608) 266-8609 Fax: (608) 267-0644

Wyoming
Administrative Div. / Dept. of Commerce / 2301 Central Ave. / Barrett
Bldg., 3rd Fl. / Cheyenne, WY 82002 / Phone: (307) 777-6300

District of Columbia
Occupational & Professional Licensing Admin., DCRA / 614 H St.,
NW, Rm. 931 / Washington, DC 20001 / Phone: (202) 727-7480

WORLD WIDE WEB & INTERNET RESOURCES

Following is an alphabetical list of associations, organizations and various other groups that are of special interest to seniors. These include
non-profit groups, government agencies and private organizations. Web
sites are given for each, however, mailing addresses and phone numbers
are also listed if available.

Access America For Seniors
http://www.seniors.gov/
Access America for Seniors provides access to many services important
to senior Americans including: getting an estimate of your Social
Security benefits, getting a verification of the Social Security benefits
that you received and comparing nursing homes and Medicare options.
Access America for Seniors also provides links to both government and
non-government web sites that contain information and services that
cover issues like: Social Security benefits, health and nutrition, consumer protection, employment and volunteer activities, taxes, travel and
leisure and education and training.

Alzheimer's Association
http://www.alz.org/
919 North Michigan Avenue, Suite 1000 / Chicago, IL 60611
phone: (312) 335-8700 / fax: (312) 335-1110 / TTY: (312) 335-8882
toll-free: 1-800-272-3900

The Alzheimer's Association is a voluntary organization that funds public education programs and provides supportive services to patients and families coping with Alzheimer's disease, including a toll-free 24-hour hotline which provides information about Alzheimer's disease and referrals to local chapters which are familiar with community resources. The Association also funds research to find a cure for Alzheimer's disease. Publications include a newsletter and education materials (in English and Spanish).

Alzheimer's Disease Education and Referral Center
http://www.alzheimers.org/
P.O. Box 8250 / Silver Spring, MD 20907-8250
phone: (301) 495-3311 / fax: (301) 495-3334
toll-free: 1-800-438-4380 / e-mail: adear@alzheimers.org

A service of the National Institute on Aging, The Alzhei-mer's Disease Education and Referral Center provides information on diagnosis and treatment, research and available services to health professionals, patients and their families and the public. A list of publications, which includes a quarterly newsletter and educational materials, is available upon request.

American Association of Retired Persons (AARP)
http://www.aarp.org/
601 E Street, N.W.
Washington, DC 20049
phone: (202) 434-2277
toll-free: 1-800-424-3410

A nonprofit organization, AARP strives to help senior Americans achieve lives of independence, dignity and purpose through services including: educational programs on topics like consumer protection and crime prevention; auto, life and home insurance programs; and an investment and annuity program. Publications include *The AARP Bulletin* (monthly), *Modern Maturity* (bi-monthly) and others on a range of topics like health, travel and money management. Local chapters are listed in the telephone directory.

American Health Care Association
http://www.ahca.org/
1201 L Street, N.W. / Washington, DC 20005
phone: (202) 842-4444 / Fax: (202) 842-3860

     The American Health Care Association (AHCA) is a professional organization that represents the interests of licensed nursing homes and assisted living care facilities to Congress, Federal regulatory agencies and other professional groups. The Association's monthly publications are for members, however, AHCA also offers educational and consumer materials on long-term care to the public.

American Parkinson's Disease Association
http://www.apdaparkinson.com/
1250 Hylan Boulevard, Suite 4B / Staten Island, NY 10305
phone: (718) 981-8001 / fax: (718) 981-4399
toll-free: 1-800-223-2732

     The American Parkinson's Disease Association is a volunteer organization that funds research to find a cure for Parkinson's disease, provides information and education to the public and offers assistance to patients and their families. The toll-free hotline links callers to local chapters and referral centers that provide information about community services, local doctor referrals and the latest treatments. Publications include education materials on the disease and related topics including speech therapy, exercise, diet and aids for daily living.

American Red Cross
http://www.redcross.org/
430 17th Street, N.W. / Washington, DC 20006
phone: (202) 737-8300

     The American Red Cross offers health programs and services, blood services and disaster and emergency relief services to the Armed Forces. Local chapters (listed in the telephone directory) offer a number of programs of special interest to seniors, including crime prevention instruction, safety education courses (e.g. boating safety, swimming, first aid, CPR) and health screening clinics. Publications on a range of topics are available from local chapters.

American Society on Aging
http://www.asaging.org/
833 Market Street, Suite 511 / San Francisco, CA 94103
phone: (415) 974-9600 / Fax: (415) 974-0300
toll-free: 1-800-537-9728 / e-mail: info@asa.asaging.org

The American Society on Aging (ASA) is a nonprofit, membership organization that informs the public and health professionals about issues affecting the quality of life for seniors and works to promote innovative ways to make improvements. Publications include *Generations* (quarterly) and *Aging Today* (bi-monthly).

Arthritis Foundation
http://www.arthritis.org/
1330 West Peachtree Street
Atlanta, GA 30309
(404) 872-7100
toll-free: 1-800-283-7800

The Arthritis Foundation is a nonprofit, volunteer organization that supports research to prevent and find a cure for arthritis, offers continuing education seminars to health professionals and aims to improve the quality of life for and represent the needs of people living with arthritis. Nationwide local chapters provide information and referral services and programs that cover issues like health, exercise, aquatic programs and support groups. Publications include brochures, videotapes and other resources (for free or at a minimal cost) and the Foundation's national consumer magazine.

Children of Aging Parents
http://www.careguide.net/careguide.cgi/caps/capshome.htm!
1609 Woodbourne Road, Suite 302-A / Levittown, PA 19057
phone: (215) 945-6900 / fax: (215) 945-8720
toll-free: 1-800-227-7294

Children of Aging Parents (CAPS) is a nonprofit organization that serves as an information clearinghouse on resources and issues dealing with seniors and provides emotional support to their caregivers as well as local referrals via the toll-free hotline. Educational services include "Instant Aging Workshops" to help the public understand the special needs of seniors and training programs for health professionals who work with the elderly. Publications include informational materials and a bi-monthly member newsletter, *Capsule.*

Consumer Information Center
http://www.pueblo.gsa.gov/
P.O. Box 100
Pueblo, CO 81009

The Consumer Information Center, a program of the General Services Administration, helps Federal Government agencies promote and distribute useful information to the public. The Center publishes the Consumer Information Catalog four times a year, which lists more than 200 selected Federal Government publications on topics of interest to consumers including automobiles, housing, nutrition, money management, employment and education.

Department of Veteran Affairs
http://www.va.gov/
810 Vermont Avenue, N.W. / Washington, DC 20420
phone: (202) 273-5700
toll-free: 1-800-827-1000 (for veterans to call in for disability claims)

The Department of Veteran Affairs (VA) provides benefits to veterans of military services and their eligible dependents including educational assistance, vocational rehabilitation, home loan guarantee programs, comprehensive dental and medical care for eligible veterans and burial benefits. The Veterans Assistance Service offers information and helps veterans, their dependents and beneficiaries apply for VA benefits. The Department's publication, *Federal Benefits for Veterans and Dependents* describes VA medical, compensation, pension, educational, loan and other insurance benefits.

Foundation for Hospice and Home Care
http://www.nahc.org/
228 7th Street, N.E. / Washington, DC 20003
phone: (202) 547-7424 / fax: (202) 547-3540

The Foundation for Hospice and Home Care promotes hospice and home care by establishing responsible standards of care, developing programs for the preparation of caregivers, educating the public, conducting research on related issues and compiling statistics on the hospice and home care industries. Educational services include administering an accreditation program and conducting annual seminars and conferences to educate caregivers. Publications include the *Directory of Accredited/Approved Home Care Aides Services* (updated biannually) and free consumer guides like *All About Homecare* and *A Consumer's Guide to Hospice Care.*

Gray Panthers
http://www.graypanthers.org/
733 15th Street, N.W., Suite 437 / Washington, DC 20005
phone: (202) 737-6637 / fax: (202) 737-1160
toll-free: 1-800-280-5362

Gray Panthers, an advocacy and educational organization, works for social change via issues such as national health care, job security, housing and education. Local chapters organize young people and seniors to work together on Gray Panther issues. The *NETWORK Newsletter* is distributed bi-monthly to members and subscribers. A list of publications is available upon request.

Centers for Medicare and Medicaid Services
http://www.cms.hhs.gov/
7500 Security Boulevard / Baltimore, MD 21244-1850
phone: (410) 786-2165
Medicare Hotline (toll-free): 1-800-638-6833

The Health Care Financing Administration (HCFA) coordinates the Federal Government's participation in Medicare and State government's administration of Medicaid. HCFA sets requirements for Medicare recipient eligibility, develops claims procedures for health care providers, regulates the contractors that process Medicare claims and maintains the toll-free Medicare Hotline. Publications include *The Medicare Handbook* and *Guide to Health Insurance for People on Medicare Financing Review* (both published yearly).

Meals on Wheels Association of America
http://www.projectmeal.org/
1414 Prince Street, Suite 202 / Alexandria, VA 22314
phone: (703) 548-8024 / fax: (703) 548-8024
e-mail: mowaa@tbg.dgsys.com

Meals on Wheels Association of America provides education, training and development opportunities to those who provide meal services to people in need. Services provided to members include: workshops on a range of topics such as fundraising, volunteer recruitment and nutrition; program insurance; and information on trends. Publications include an annual member directory and the quarterly *MOWAA News magazine* and *MOWAA Notice newsletter*.

The National Aging Information Center
http://www.aoa.gov/naic/
Administration on Aging
330 Independence Avenue, S.W., Rm. 4656 / Washington, DC 20201
phone: (202) 619-7501 / fax: (202) 401-7620
e-mail: naic@ban-gate.aoa.dhhs.gov

The National Aging Information Center (NAIC) established by the Administration on Aging, serves as a source of aging information by developing, maintaining and providing access to databases that include information on: Older Americans Act Title IV research and demonstration products; Administration on Aging and other aging-related publications; resources on services provided to seniors by Federal programs; and statistics on senior Americans.

National Association for Home Care
http://www.nahc.org/
228 7th Street, S.E. / Washington, DC 20003
phone: (202) 547-7424 / fax: (202) 547-3540
The National Association for Home Care (NAHC) is a professional organization that represents agencies providing home care services (e.g. home health agencies, hospice programs and homemaker/home health aid agencies). NAHC helps develop professional standards for such agencies, offers continuing education programs to agency staff and monitors State and Federal legislation that affects home care services. Publications include the member monthlies, *Caring Magazine*, *Home Care News* and *NAHC Reports*.

National Association of State Units on Aging
http://www.nasua.org/
1225 I Street, N.W., Suite 725 / Washington, DC 20005
phone: (202) 898-2578 / fax: (202) 898-2583
e-mail: staff@nasua.org
The National Association of State Units on Aging (NASUA) is a public interest group that promotes social policy at the State and National levels to serve the needs of seniors. NASUA provides information (e.g. reports on current legislative issues), training and technical assistance and professional development support to its members. Publications are available on many topics, including the Older Americans Act, long-term care, older worker issues and elder abuse.

National Cancer Institute

http://www.nci.nih.gov/

Office of Cancer Communications / Building 31, Room 10A07

31 Center Drive MSC 2580 / Bethesda, MD 20892-2580

phone: (301) 496-5583

toll-free (cancer information): 1-800-4-CANCER (1-800-422-6237)

The National Cancer Institute (NCI), funds cancer research and educates the public on cancer. Education efforts include: a national campaign targeting people age sixty-five and older and their health professionals; the toll-free Cancer Information hotline which provides up-to-date information and local resources; and publications on specific types of cancer, prevention, detection, diagnosis, treatment, coping and survivorship. *The Journal of the National Cancer Institute* is published monthly for health professionals.

National Center on Elder Abuse

http://www.elderabusecenter.org/

Research and Demonstration Dept. / American Public Welfare Assoc.

201 15th Street NW, Suite 350 / Washington, DC 20005

phone: (202) 898-2578 / fax: (202) 898-2583

Operated jointly with the National Association of State Units on Aging, the National Committee for the Prevention of Elder Abuse and the University of Delaware, the Center serves the knowledge and skills development needs of professionals concerned with elder abuse/neglect, through services like: technical assistance, information about the best practices in the field and studies on training and research. Publications include: *Elder Abuse: Questions and Answers – an Information Guide for Professionals and Concerned Citizens*; *An Analysis of State Laws Addressing Elder Abuse, Neglect and Exploitation*; and the *NCEA Exchange* newsletter.

National Committee to Preserve Social Security and Medicare
http://www.ncpssm.org/
10 G Street, N.E., Suite 600 / Washington, DC 20002-4215
phone: (202) 216-0420 / fax: (202) 216-0451
Senior Flash Hotline (toll-free): 1-800-998-0180

    The National Committee to Preserve Social Security and Medicare, an advocacy and education organization, is dedicated to protecting Federal programs vital to seniors' well-being by lobbying Congress, through letter and postcard campaigns and via public relations efforts to influence lawmakers. Publications include free informational brochures, an annual report and a bi-monthly member magazine, *Secure Retirement, the Newsmagazine for Mature Americans.*

The National Council on the Aging, Inc.
http://www.ncoa.org/
409 3rd Street, S.W., Suite 200 / Washington, DC 20024
phone: (202) 479-1200 / fax: (202) 479-0735
e-mail: info@ncoa.org

    The National Council on the Aging (NCOA) is a private, nonprofit organization that seeks to promote the well-being of seniors and enhance the field of aging. NCOA also provides information, training, technical assistance, advocacy and leadership through its information center, demonstrations, research and library. Publications include *Perspective on Aging* (magazine), *NCOA Networks* (newsletter) and materials on topics of interest to senior Americans.

National Diabetes Information Clearinghouse
http://www.niddk.nih.gov/
1 Information Way / Bethesda, MD 20892-3560
phone: (301) 654-3327 / fax: (301) 907-8906
e-mail: ndic@info.niddk.nih.gov

    The National Diabetes Information Clearinghouse (NDIC) provides information about diabetes through its publications to patients,

health professionals and the public and offers referrals to diabetes organizations, including support groups.

National Institute on Aging
http://www.nih.gov/nia/
Public Information Office / Building 31, Room 5C27
31 Center Drive MSC 2292 / Bethesda, MD 20892-2292
phone: (301) 496-1752 / fax: (301) 496-1072
toll-free: 1-800-222-2225 / e-mail: niainfo@access.digex.net

The National Institute on Aging (NIA) conducts and supports
biomedical, social and behavioral research related to aging processes
and diseases. Current research projects affiliated with NIA include: The
Baltimore Longitudinal Study of Aging (follows the same people over
a long period of time to study aging's effect on health) and studies of
new methods of diagnosing and treating Alzheimer's disease (NIA funds
the Alzheimer's Disease Education and Referral Center). Publications
include free materials on a range of aging-related topics.

National Long-Term Care Ombudsman Resource Center
http://www.nccnhr.org/
National Citizens' Coalition for Nursing Home Reform
1424 16th Street, N.W., Suite 202 / Washington, DC 20036
phone: (202) 332-2275 / fax: (202) 332-2949

The Resource Center supports the ongoing development and
operation of federally mandated nationwide long-term care ombudsman programs. These programs investigate and try to resolve the problems experienced by long-term care residents. With the National
Association of State Units on Aging, The Center provides training, consultation, technical assistance and resource materials to ombudsman
programs. Their newsletter, *InfoBulletin*, is available on request.

National Long-Term Care Resource Center
http://www.hsr.umn.edu/
Institute for Health Services Research
University of Minnesota School of Public Health
420 Delaware Street / Box 197 Mayo / Minneapolis, MN 55455
phone: (612) 624-5171 / fax: (612) 624-5434
An effort of the University of Minnesota Institute for Health
Services Research and the National Academy of State Health Policy,
The Center assists the aging network to develop, administer, monitor
and refine community-based long-term care systems reform.

National Organization for Victim Assistance
http://www.try-nova.org/
1757 Park Road, N.W. / Washington, DC 20010
phone: (202) 232-6682 / fax: (202) 462-2255
e-mail: nova@access.digex.net
The National Organization for Victim Assistance (NOVA), a private, nonprofit group, aids victims of violent crime and disaster through
its services: 24-hour crisis counseling, referrals to support services, information on victim assistance/ laws in each state, training and technical
support and government lobbying for victims' rights. Besides the *NOVA*
Newsletter (free for members, $3 for non-members) educational mate-
rials like *The Elder Crime Victim* are available.

National Policy and Resource Center on Nutrition and Aging
http://www.fiu.edu/~nutreldr/
Dept. of Dietetics and Nutrition / Florida International Institute
University Park, OE200 / Miami, FL 33199
phone: (305) 348-1517 / fax: (305)348-1518
e-mail: nutrelder@solix.fiu.edu
The Center works with the Administration on Aging to improve
the nutrition of senior Americans mostly through information dissemina-
tion, the development of a public outreach campaign, training, technical

assistance and policy analysis for agencies and organizations involved in the fields of aging and nutrition.

National Stroke Association
http://www.stroke.org/
96 Inverness Drive East, Suite I / Englewood, CO 80112-5112
phone: (303) 649-9299 / fax: (303) 649-1328

The National Stroke Association provides information on the prevention, detection and treatment of stroke, aftercare, rehabilitation and self-help services. The Association also offers supportive services to stroke survivors and their families. Publications include *Be Stroke Smart* (monthly) and materials on stroke related issues.

Robert Wood Johnson Foundation
http://www.rwjf.org/
Route 1 North College Road East / Princeton, NJ 08543-2316
phone: (609) 452-8701

A private, philanthropic organization, the Foundation aims to improve the health and health care of all Americans. Among the issues focused upon are the rising cost of health care and improving basic health services as well as services for those who suffer from chronic conditions. Publications of the Foundation include a quarterly newsletter, *Advances*, an annual report and an informational brochure.

SeniorNet
http://www.seniornet.org/
One Kearny Street, 3rd Level / San Francisco, CA 94108
phone: (415) 352-1210
toll-free: 1-800-747-6848 / e-mail: seniornet@aol.com

SeniorNet is a nonprofit educational organization founded to teach computer skills to and provide seniors with access to information and an online community. Members receive: discounts on computer products, an online account and a subscription to the *SeniorNet Newsletter* and *Sourcebook*. Other publications on computer-related topics of interest to seniors are available.

The Skin Cancer Foundation
http://www.skincancer.org/
245 Fifth Avenue / New York, NY 10016
phone: (212) 725-5751 / e-mail: info@skincancer.org
toll-free: 1-800-SKIN-490 (1-800-754-6490)

The Skin Cancer Foundation, a nonprofit, public information organization, promotes public awareness of skin cancer and provides support for medical training and research. Publications include brochures and posters that warn of the dangers of sun exposure and describe symptoms, diagnosis and treatment of skin cancer. To receive a list of materials, send a self-addressed, stamped envelope.

Social Security Administration
http://www.ssa.gov/
6401 Security Boulevard / Baltimore, MD 21235
phone: (410) 965-7700 / fax: (410) 965-0695
toll-free (information): 1-800-772-1213

The Social Security Administration (SSA) manages Social Security benefits as well as the Supplemental Security Income (SSI) program. The SSA pays benefits to retired or disabled workers and their dependants, as well as to eligible survivors of deceased workers. SSI payments are made to those who are blind, disabled or sixty-five years or older with limited incomes or resources. SSA offices, located in every state, are listed in the telephone directory under "Social Security Administration" or "U.S. Government" and provide *Understanding Social Security* and other publications.

United Way of America
http: www.unitedway.org/
701 North Fairfax Street / Alexandria, VA 22314-2045
phone: (703) 836-7100 / fax: (703) 683-7813
toll-free (information services): 1-800-UWA-2757

The United Way of America is an association of local, independent United Way agencies across the United States, funded through charitable donations and social service and public assistance programs.

Local agencies are listed in the telephone directory. To receive a list of publications, including the videos, *The Graying of America* and *United Way and You*, call 1-800-772-0008.

Visiting Nurse Association of America
http://www.vnaa.org/
11 Beacon Street, Suite 910 / Boston, MA 02108
phone: (617) 523-4042 / fax: (610) 227-4843
toll-free: 1-888-866-8773

Visiting Nurse Associations are community-supported nonprofit providers of home health care to patients of all ages, regardless of their ability to pay. In addition to home care, they operate adult day care centers, wellness clinics, hospices and meals on wheels programs and offer services such as physical, speech and occupational therapy and nutritional counseling. Information about Visiting Nurse Associations is available upon request.

Volunteers of America
http://www.voa.org/
110 South Union Street / Alexandria, VA 22314
phone: (703) 548-2288 / fax: (703) 687-1972
toll-free: 1-800-899-0089

Volunteers of America (VOA), a nonprofit organization, offers programs and services to meet the needs of a local community. Programs and services specifically for seniors include senior centers, home repair services, homemaker assistance, meals-on-wheels and transportation programs, foster grandparent and senior volunteer programs, adult day care, affordable housing and nursing home care. Publications include *The Volunteers Gazette* (quarterly) and *Spirit*, VOA's magazine (three times per year).

Emergency Contact Information

Name: _____

Street Address: _____

City: _____ State: _____ Zip Code _____

Phone: (H) _____ (Cell) _____

Email Address: _____ Marital Status: _____

Phone: (H) _____ (Cell) _____

Date of Birth: _____ Social Security # _____

If married, name of spouse: _____

Health Insurance Information

Medicare #_____

Medicare Supplement policy # _____

Medicare Managed Care Company and # _____

Long-Term Care Insurance Company and # _____

Doctors

Primary Physician and phone # _____

Physician Specialist and phone #_____

Physician Specialist and phone #_____

Pharmacy

Name of Pharmacy:_____   Phone # _____

Street Address: _____

City: _____   State: _____   Zip Code _____

Prescriptions and Medications

Medication	Dosage	Frequency	Prescribing Doctor
_____	_____	_____	_____
_____	_____	_____	_____
_____	_____	_____	_____
_____	_____	_____	_____
_____	_____	_____	_____
_____	_____	_____	_____
_____	_____	_____	_____

Emergency Contact List

Name: _____

Street Address: _____

City: _____ State: _____ Zip Code _____

Phone: (H) _____ (Cell) _____

Relationship: _____

Name: _____

Street Address: _____

City: _____ State: _____ Zip Code _____

Phone: (H) _____ (Cell) _____

Relationship: _____

Name: _____

Street Address: _____

City: _____ State: _____ Zip Code _____

Phone: (H) _____ (Cell) _____

Relationship: _____

Hospital of Choice

Name: _____

Street Address: _____

City: _____ State: _____ Zip Code _____

Phone: (H) _____ (Website) _____

Recent Hospitalizations

Name of Hospital: _____

Reason Treated: _____ Date From/To: _____

Name and phone # of doctor: _____

Name of Hospital: _____

Reason Treated: _____ Date From/To: _____

Name and phone # of doctor: _____

Name of Hospital: _____

Reason Treated: _____ Date From/To: _____

Name and phone # of doctor: _____